THE ULTIMATE GUIDE TO MASTER YOUR MEMORY

Jayasimha, popularly known as Squadron Leader R. Jayasimha, is India's leading trainer in memory and soft skills. The only Indian to hold the maximum number of Guinness Records in the world and the president of the World Memory Sports Council for India, he has been conducting National Memory Championships every year in the country to encourage raw talent. He has also featured in the reality TV show *Fear Factor Extreme: Khatron ke Khiladi* (Season 1, 2008) in South Africa with actors Akshay Kumar and Pooja Bedi.

Author of several books, Jayasimha has 21 years of experience in the field of education, training and development in the Indian Air Force. Of the many awards and medals to his name, there is the Sword of Honour that he received from former President Sri Ramaswamy Venkataraman for the Pilots' Training at the Air Force Academy and the Chief of Air Staff Commendation' for his exemplary service in the Indian Air Force.

He lives in Kukatpally, Hyderabad.

THE ULTIMATE GUIDE TO MASTER YOUR MEMORY

Jayasimha

Published by
Rupa Publications India Pvt. Ltd 2018
7/16, Ansari Road, Daryaganj
New Delhi 110002

Sales centres:

Allahabad Bengaluru Chennai
Hyderabad Jaipur Kathmandu
Kolkata Mumbai

Copyright © Jayasimha Ravirala 2018

While every effort has been made to verify the authenticity of the information contained in this book, the publisher and the author are in no way liable for the use of the information contained in this book.

All rights reserved.
No part of this publication may be reproduced, transmitted, or stored in a retrieval system, in any form or by any means, electronic, mechanical, photocopying, recording or otherwise, without the prior permission of the publisher.

ISBN: 978-93-5304-019-2

First impression 2018

10 9 8 7 6 5 4 3 2 1

The moral right of the author has been asserted.

Printed by Thomson Press India Ltd., Faridabad

This book is sold subject to the condition that it shall not, by way of trade or otherwise, be lent, resold, hired out, or otherwise circulated, without the publisher's prior consent, in any form of binding or cover other than that in which it is published.

CONTENTS

Preface   *vii*
Introduction: Do We Use 100 Per Cent of Our Brain   *ix*

1. Improving Memory — 1
2. Principles of Memory — 6
3. Basic Association Method — 11
4. Imagination Method — 20
5. Location Method (or Method of Loci) — 26
6. Ancient Memory Methods — 30
7. Substitution Method — 49
8. Number–Shape Method — 59
9. Number–Value Method — 64
10. Number–Rhyme Method — 66
11. Body Parts Method — 71
12. House Method — 75
13. Alphabet Method — 78
14. Symbolization Method — 82
15. Consonance Method — 86
16. Mnemonic Method — 89
17. Memorizing Numbers I — 93
18. Mastering Numbers II — 104
19. Memorizing Binary Numbers — 111
20. Personalized Memory System — 115
21. Memorizing Definitions, Equations and Formuale — 123
22. Memorizing Long Speeches — 129

23. Memorizing Months and Days	134
24. Memorizing Calendars	136
25. Memorizing To-do Lists and Road Directions	140
26. Memorizing Names and Faces	144
27. Reinforcing and Reviewing	148
28. Overcoming Absent-mindedness or Forgetfulness	152
29. Erasing Bad Memories	158

Feedback Welcome   163

PREFACE

In today's world, we are relentlessly bombarded with information from countless sources. It's actually a wonder how we ever get work done, engage ourselves in something creative or remember anything meaningful. Thanks to the new-age technology that our gadgets keep ringing with incoming calls and notifications even when we are asleep or just when we wake up. It seems there is never a second to spare to take stock of daily events.

Everyone faces this challenge, be it students, professionals, businessmen, home makers or elderly people. It is a challenge of not being able to retain and recall something that they saw, heard, read or experienced over a short or long period. It has become such a common issue that people have begun to assume that they were born with a weak memory.

The Ultimate Guide to Master Your Memory is aimed to equip the reader with the tools, techniques and skills required to remember more, faster, for a long time and with least effort possible. One of the main reasons this book will be useful is that it will assist readers to set their priorities and take a stock of things important to them.

Furthermore, this book will help change our lives by enhancing memory. You will have to spend a small amount of your time every day to go over the exercises mentioned in this book and consciously apply them. They will help you organize and exercise your thoughts in a certain pattern where you retain more of important information. I am humbled by writing this book as it made me realize the power of my own mind and how important it is to constantly stretch its limitations. Creative Memory is another aspect that works on the fundamental laws and rules of memory. It goes against the regular practice of only repeating texts and writing down everything that needs to be remembered. It is visual, extremely simple and fun to use. Contestants of the Indian and World Memory Championships use many of the techniques mentioned here. At present, I am the president of the World Memory Sports Council for India. I am also training memory athletes for various championships with the help of these techniques. I can assure you that you do not have to be a genius to get started.

It is essential that you practise the techniques learnt in this book. Merely reading it will not improve your memory.

This book is simple enough to show improvements that you could easily measure the same day. People of all ages, with least effort, can learn these techniques due to the exercises provided in the book. It involves multi-sensory exercises and activities, which makes the entire brain work. Do not give up on it, yet. You have the key to unlock the mysteries of your memory!

I hope you enjoy reading and learning from this book as much as I did writing it.

INTRODUCTION: DO WE USE 100 PER CENT OF OUR BRAIN?

You may be surprised but the answer is NO!

Let's first look at the basics. The human brain weighs around 1.4 kilograms. It is about two per cent of the total body weight, but it uses 20 per cent of the oxygen inhaled for the entire body. Most of our brain cells are present since birth and the increase in weight of the brain results from the growth of these cells. During the first six years, a child learns and acquires new behavioural patterns at the fastest rate during his lifetime.

If we were meant to do manual tasks with one finger, we would NOT have been born with ten fingers. Therefore, if we were meant to use only a small percentage of our brain cells to lead a happy life, we would not have been born with 10 times as much to use. In fact, man (Homo sapiens) is the only creature on earth that does not use its 100 per cent brain capacity.

Dolphins have about the same neural capacity as human beings do and they live as intelligent, fun loving and harmonious creatures. They use their brains in its entirety, not just a fraction of it like we do. Is it too much of an imaginative stretch to assume that the more we use our brain's capacity, the more harmonious our lives would be?

In other words, we are creatures designed just as perfectly as every other creature on earth, but do not use the full potential of our brain as they do. Why? Is it because we no longer know *how* to connect with our 'energy source' like all other creatures? Or, is it that we don't care to make free *choices* to create such connects? Free will is such a confusing thing to 10 per cent brain users and is controlled by the knee-jerk reaction of the body!

Average human beings are losing over 100,000 brain cells every day due to disuse or misuse. Regardless of the reason for neglecting the brain, it's the 'use it or lose it' axiom at work here. The more a person neglects using his brain potential, the more his condition is likely to worsen. The brain is like a knife. If we don't use the knife for long, it will become blunt. Similarly, if we don't use our brain on a regular basis, the cells will slowly begin to die. This leads to absentmindedness, forgetfulness, Alzheimer's and lastly, Dementia.

So, what is the solution to this? Can we really use 100 per cent of our brains and improve the quality of our lives? Of course, we can! Instead of experiencing memory loss, we can become memory wizards.

The first step in this direction as we go through this book is to practise memory techniques.

Practise, Practise, Practise

Practice is the key to master a skill. One of the critical aspects is the fact that with practice, the demands on your attention get smaller and smaller. Interestingly, it appears that there is no limit to the improvement in this practice. Your physical condition will limit how much you can improve a practical skill, but a cognitive skill will continue to improve as long as you keep practising.

One thing that all of us need to remember is that memory is not just about techniques and methods but it has a lot to do with self-confidence. If you feel that you can do it, you will be able to do it. There is nothing special about improving memory, anyone can do it. What you will need to remember is that you must be consistent, and sincere efforts towards any self-improvement program will finally pay off. Insincere and half-hearted attempts, which end within a few weeks, do not make much of a difference.

There are no shortcuts or instant cures for anything in this world. Only persistence works. Anything is possible if you want to do it. Memory improvement is just a small drop in the ocean of self-improvement. However, this drop is very significant, because it can change your life in terms of money, status, knowledge, relationships and a horde of other things. So pull up your socks and get to work. And don't give up if you don't see significant results in a few weeks. The results will become apparent over a period. Just keep at it!

Remember to practise and challenge your memory and you will marvel at the results.

ONE

IMPROVING MEMORY

Memory is a strange thing. It can be as solid as words engraved in a stone, or it can be fluid and changeable, sometimes dangerously so. It is also one of the most essential of human powers, allowing us to make judgements, make decisions, plan and yes, even dream.

Memory is simply one of the most important functions of the brain. However, it is not perfect. It can be manipulated, edited or even *improved*. Yes! You read it right! All of us can improve our *memory*.

If our brains were computers, we would simply add a chip to upgrade our memories. However, the human brain is more complex than even the most advanced machines in the world, so we need to put in more effort to improve the human memory. Just like muscular strength, your ability to remember will increase when you exercise your memory.

What is Memory?

Simply put, memory is the mental activity of recalling information that you have learned or experienced. That simple definition, though, covers a complex process that involves many different parts of the brain and serves us in disparate ways.

Memory can be short-term or long-term. In short-term memory, your mind stores information for a few seconds or a few minutes—the time it takes you to dial a phone number you just looked up or to compare the prices of several items in a store or directions to go to a particular place. Such memory is fragile, and that is how it is meant to be. Your brain will soon read 'disk full' if you retained every phone number you ever called, every dish you ordered in a restaurant or every ad you watched on TV. Your brain holds an average of seven items, which is why you can usually remember a new phone number for a few minutes, but you will need your credit card in front of you when buying something online.

Long-term memory involves the information you make an effort (conscious or unconscious) to retain. This is because— it is something personal to you (for example, details of family members and friends), it is important (such as job procedures or materials you're studying for a test), or it has made an emotional impression (a movie of your favourite hero that you had enjoyed, your first salary, the first prize you won at school, the first time you ever caught a fish, the day your uncle died). Some information that you store as long-term memory requires a conscious effort to recall—episodic memories, which are personal memories about experiences you have had at specific times; and semantic memories (factual data that is not bound by time or place), which can be anything from the names of the planets to the colour of your child's hair. Another type of long-term memory is procedural memory, which involves skills and routines you perform so often that they do not require conscious recalling.

The Importance of Memory

Memory is life and life is memory. Imagine for a minute that you have forgotten who you are, what you are and where you need to go. It will be so confusing for you. Without memory, our life will become like a vegetable.

Most of the schools and colleges are forcing children to use rote memory. This age-old method accompanied by increased competition, unreasonable expectations from parents and unhealthy competition among private schools to acquire higher ranks and marks is further pressurizing the youngsters.

This is leading a lot of students to commit suicides, or just become ordinary job seekers.

One must learn these memory techniques and practise Memory Sports on a regular basis to explore their innate potential.

Hence, there is a need for all of us to train ourselves in the latest and most creative methods of learning. This will help us understand how our brain functions and ways to enhance creativity.

Why Memory Sports?

There are world championships for every physical sport like swimming, boxing, football, cricket, hockey, athletics and so on. Yet, there is no such championship for the most important cognitive function of all without which none of the others will exist—*Memory.* The World Memory Sports Council was formed in the early nineties by Tony Buzan and Raymond Kenee in UK. Its aim was to conduct memory championships every year in different countries and have a World Memory Championship for all these athletes. This was done to inculcate a habit of practising memory as a sport.

The World Memory Sports Council of India was formed in 2008. This book provides techniques some of which feature in Memory Sports organized by the World Memory Sports Council across the globe every year. These techniques will help the readers not only in their day-to-day lives, but will also help in case some of you are interested in participating in and winning the memory competitions.

Can Memory be Really Improved?

Yes, we can indeed improve our Memory. Memory doesn't completely depend on our heredity. Twenty per cent of our brain health depends on heredity and the remaining 80 per cent of it is a skill. The latter is something that we can learn and perfect through practice. There is nothing called good memory or bad memory. We only have trained or untrained memory. Through proper training, anyone can improve his or her memory. Our brain is similar to a gadget, a machine or an instrument. If we are able to get an instructions, manual to learn the techniques and practise them, we will be able to use our brain as we use any other machine. My endeavour is to help you with those simple techniques, which will make a big difference in your ability to remember and recall.

Certain areas of the brain are especially important to form and retain memory:

1. The hippocampus, a primitive structure deep in the brain, plays the single largest role to process information as memory.
2. The amygdala, an almond-shaped area near the hippocampus, processes emotions and helps imprint memories that involve emotions.
3. The cerebral cortex, the outer layer of the brain, stores most long-term memory in different zones, depending on what kind of processing the information requires—language, sensory input, problem solving and so forth.
4. In addition, memory involves communication among the brain's network of neurons.

Stages of Memory Foundation and Maintenance

There are three stages the brain undergoes to form and retain memories. These are explained in the table below:

Reception	Storage	Recall
New information enters the brain along pathways between neurons. The key to encode the information into your memory is concentration. Unless you intently focus on the available information, it is heard/seen but is quickly forgotten. This is why teachers keep nagging students about paying attention.	If you concentrate well enough to encode new information into your brain, the hippocampus sends a signal to store the information as long-term memory. This happens more easily if the information relates to something you already know or it stimulates an emotional response.	When you need to recall information, your brain has to activate the same pattern of nerve cells it used to store that information. The more frequently you need the information, the easier it is to retrieve it through the healthy nerves.

TWO

PRINCIPLES OF MEMORY

Everyone wants to learn ways to enhance memory, but they do not know how to go about it. Hence, one needs to start from the basics. Fundamentally, memory is a skill, it follows a process, and there are a few underlying principles. One needs to have an 'interest' in the matter that he or she wants to remember. No matter where our interests lie, the brain automatically remembers things related to them. Imagine a scenario where you love cricket and you are a big fan of Virat Kohli. The brain will remember all the details related to the number of centuries made by the cricketer, including the details of his wedding. Similarly, if you want to remember academics, you should take interest in that particular field of study and your brain will automatically remember the required information.

Most importantly, there has to be a purpose, aim or a goal. The brain should know why it should remember what it is trying to remember. What are the benefits of remembering a particular data or information? If the brain knows 'why' the information is essential, it will automatically try to remember it. That is because the memory function of the brain is based on three fundamental principles of memory.

1. Association
2. Imagination
3. Location

If these are put to work together, they can be used to generate powerful memories with techniques inclusive of these principles.

Association Method

Memory is nothing but learning something new and connecting it to something that we already know. As a baby first remembers his or her mother's face, then her voice, her touch and so on, we too form the base of our memory in the same manner. Once we form the base memory, whatever we learn hereafter is connected to what we already know. This is called Association.

Association is the method by which you link what is to be remembered with something personal. The association will automatically remind us about the memorized object if we can place it on top of the associated object, wrap them around each other, link them together, merge them, rotate them around each other or make them dance together.

For example, remember the following objects in relation to each other.

Elephant	–	Telephone
Butterfly	–	School
Peanut	–	Bird
Aeroplane	–	Refrigerator
Bike	–	Fire
Tiger	–	Kite
Fan	–	River
Apple	–	Tree
Pen	–	Chair

Whenever you need to remember objects with respect to each other, you could associate them in the following manner—an *elephant* is speaking over the *telephone*, a *butterfly* is going to school, *peanuts* are being eaten by a *bird*, an *aeroplane* is carrying a *refrigerator*, and so on.

We need to visualize these scenarios in our brain, magnify them and conjure their presence.

You may do the same exercise for the remaining objects to associate them to each other.

Imagination Method

Imagination plays a very important role in Memory. The more vivid and funny the imagination is, the better and easier will be the chances to recall them. The whole mechanism of Memory revolves around imagination. We can make up one funny story.

Take for instance these objects below:

butterfly, cow, tree, bike, fish, film, dog, towel, mountain, doctor, tennis

Let us imagine that a colourful *butterfly* is sitting on a white *cow*. The *cow* is climbing a big banyan *tree*. A white Duke *bike* is mounted atop the *tree* and a *fish* is riding the bike to watch the *film Sholay*. In the film, you see a *dog* running in a pink *towel*. The dog falls over a big *mountain*. It injures itself and calls for a *doctor* who instead of treating it is busy playing *tennis*.

Once we imagine the sequence of events in this funny way and connect one to the other, it will enable us to remember the objects in sequence easily. This is a very powerful memory method.

By using this method, besides Memory, we enhance our creativity, which is the basic essence of life's success.

Location Method

Location technique is a little different from the imagination technique. In the imagination method, we have been connecting one object to the other by some vivid imagination. Contrarily, the location technique works independently, i.e., we don't connect two objects with each other. In this method, we will have some permanent locations. Thereafter, we will connect the objects to be remembered with the permanent location.

First, we should have different locations in a house or an office that we visit frequently or any other place that is familiar. Imagine, I have my house and in it there are a few locations that I am familiar with in a sequence.

> *bed, ceiling fan, cupboard, television, foot mat, washroom, bedroom door, the fencing, tree, treadmill, washing machine, stairs, puja room, kitchen, refrigerator, dining table, sofa set, exit door.*

First, I have fixed these locations in a proper order. I go through the locations many times so that I am able to recall the sequence easily.

Now, I need you to remember the following list of objects:

laptop, apple, cockroach, mobile, spectacles, tube light, Rahul Gandhi, Jurassic Park, ice cream, Marina Beach, Ayyappan, Tihar Jail, etc.

To remember these objects in sequence, what we need to do is associate them with the permanent locations that we already have.

> Such as, the *bed* has *laptops* spread all over it.
> From the *ceiling fans*, *apples* are falling.
> The *cupboard* is full of *cockroaches*.
> On the *television*, an ad for *mobiles* is being shown.
> A *foot mat* is wearing *spectacles*.
> In the *washroom*, *Rahul Gandhi* is taking a bath.
> As we open the *bedroom door*, it is leading us to the *Jurassic Park*.
> On the *fencing*, *ice creams* are placed.

Climbing the *tree*, you will be able to see the *Marina Beach*.
On the *treadmill*, *Ayyappan* is running.
Washing machines are being provided to every inmate of *Tihar Jail*, etc.

You may create a list of words to remember and then it practise yourself.

In this way, we keep associating the objects or the words to be remembered with the fixed locations. The moment we see the fixed locations, we will be able to recall the associated object with it.

The advantage of this method over the imagination method is that in the latter, if we miss one object or the story link breaks, it is difficult to recollect the next one. In the location method, however, the objects are easier to recall since it is only the locations that are connected to the objects. In case we forget one association, we will still remember the next location and object. Hence this is slightly easier and more powerful a method than the imagination method.

THREE

BASIC ASSOCIATION METHOD

In the Chapter 3, we have learnt the techniques of Association, Imagination and Location in brief. Let us further master the Association technique as this is the foundation for all memory techniques that we are about to learn.

Associations, Associations and Nothing but Associations...

The basic method of memory is the association method and it is an extremely strong one. Memory is nothing but associating something that you don't know with something that you do, or simply, connecting the new to the old. If you had to remember somebody's address as 1225 Memory Lane, wouldn't it be easier to remember Christmas (12-25/December 25th) than four separate numbers? Now you have something that is meaningful. You can take your storytelling technique and associate it to Memory. It may take some imagination, but that just comes with practice.

Another strong point of the Association technique is that it allows you to utilize information you already know.

People tend to forget the third type of information. Ancient wizards used to say that information about everything always exists everywhere. They neither referred to words, images, phone numbers and dates, nor did they mean objects that our brains reflect upon. What they meant by the term 'information' was in fact 'associations'.

Thus, the first information type is associations, formed between objects, phenomena and surrounding world events. Indeed, such information exists everywhere, always and about everything one can ever possibly imagine.

Leaves grow on tree branches; the sun is always in the sky; fish swim in the sea. If there is lightning, expect thunder; if it rains, clothes get wet. Speech construction involving 'if... then...', reflects the analysed information type—associations. 'If branch, then leaves'; 'if sugar, then sweet'; 'if fire, then smoke'.

This kind of information is very important for us since our brain memorizes only this. Your brain memorizes the associations. When you see a vase with a rose in it on a table, your brain remembers the connection between 'vase,' 'rose' and 'table'. The brain does not memorize the images itself.

Where does our brain get memories from then? Do we still remember words or images?

We encounter simple examples of memory principles every day in a kitchen. Why do you remove your hand when you touch a hot kettle? What a silly question, you might say. This reaction does not just happen. It is the heat stimulating the skin receptors to produce an *association* that signals you to pull your hand away automatically. Image reproduction works in the same way. When you see a vase, it acts upon your eyes and an *association* signals your brain to produce images of the 'rose' and the 'table'. Similarly, when you hear a 'cat', it acts upon your ears and an *association* forms an image of a cat in your mind.

The brain is not the information warehouse we think it is. It can only generate *associations*. With respect to any other type of information (words, images, music, phone numbers, etc.), the brain is only a generator of information. A 'generator of information' sounds peculiar, but it is exactly the kind of device you have in your minds.

Analogically, no one will possibly ever try to find electricity in an electric generator. We all know that a generator *creates* electric energy. An attempt to find images, words or phone numbers stored in the brain is futile—they are not in your mind; your brain generates them.

For the electric generator to create electric energy, it needs to be rotated. For the brain to begin creating images and words, it needs to receive signals (stimuli). Huge varieties of stimuli go to the brain and agitate previously created connections according to which the brain creates (generates) as information: images, words or movements.

The most primitive type of association, a reflex, is familiar to all of us. For a reflex to work, a stimulus is necessary. Human memory works according to 'Stimulus-Reaction' (S-R) principle.

From this simple example, you can see that an attempt to memorize phone numbers and historical dates in their usual appearance is an absolutely senseless thing to do. The brain is not capable of doing this in vast quantities. It is necessary to learn to memorize the associations that exist in phone numbers and historical dates. Using these associations, our brain will generate the necessary data.

We can draw a conclusion based on the fact that the brain is only capable of creating associations—the brain will not generate information if an incoming stimulating signal is not received making this retention process impossible. The reflex of pulling your hand away will not work unless you touch something hot. You will not sneeze unless a speck of dust enters your nose. You may have no idea of the innate genetic reaction programs you have unless you encounter a certain stimulating situation.

I am now going to give you a list of 20 items and you are going to try to *recall* them. I want you to memorize this list in this *exact* order. The only rule is to go through this list *once* and spend *no more* than five to seven seconds on each item. Sit back, relax, clear your mind and remember; don't write this down.

1. Stick
2. Spectacles
3. Auto
4. Tiger
5. 5 Star chocolate
6. Cricket
7. Rainbow
8. Hourglass
9. Planets of Solar System
10. Fingers
11. Railway track
12. Bananas
13. Unlucky number
14. Valentine's Day
15. Indian flag
16. Abraham Lincoln
17. Magazine
18. Voter card
19. Potassium
20. Shotgun

Now, get a sheet of paper and write down the items you remember. How did you fare? Did you get all 20? Probably not. Most people manage to remember between three and five items. If you got six or more, that's great! More than 10 items, is definitely above average!

The above exercise has three applications: first, it is simply a memory test to provide us with a starting point. Second, every item on the list can actually be associated with a number. Third, the list above will help you start the process of association, which is equivalent to the first step in memory training.

The list provided below is an example of basic association. Let me show you what I mean.

- Number 1 is a stick. Number one looks like stick.
- Number 2 stands for spectacles. These spectacles cover a pair of eyes.
- Number 3 is an auto. An auto has three wheels.
- Number 4 is a tiger. A tiger will have four legs.
- Number 5 is a 5 Star chocolate. A 5 Star chocolate is basically a thing that we associate with number 5.
- Number 6 is cricket. Sixes are being hit in cricket and spectators like them very much.
- Number 7 is a rainbow. There are seven colours in a rainbow. The acronym VIBGYOR basically represents 7 colours of a rainbow.
- Number 8 is an hourglass and eight resembles the shape of an hourglass.
- Number 9 is planets of the solar system. There are nine planets in the solar system.
- Number 10 is fingers. We have ten fingers and ten toes.
- Number 11 is a railway track. The railway track looks like No. 11.
- Number 12 is bananas. A dozen bananas will have 12 pieces of the fruit.
- Number 13 is an unlucky number. People do associate something unlucky with No. 13.
- Number 14 is associated with Valentine's Day. Valentine's Day is on 14 February.
- Number 15 is the Indian Flag. India got its independence on 15 August, right?
- Number 16 is a Abraham Lincoln. Abraham Lincoln was

the 16th President of United States of America.
- Number 17 is a magazine. Now, some of you may not know that there is a magazine for teenage girls called *Seventeen*.
- Number 18 is voter card. When someone turns 18, he or she is eligible to vote and is issued a voter card.
- Number 19 is Potassium. Potassium is the 19th element in the Periodic Table.
- Number 20 is a shotgun—a 20-gauge shotgun.

This list was created using the first level of memory training called Association. It works. Seldom did we associate nine with the nine planets of the solar system. It would not work if number three was appointed to planets. Basic association does play a significant role in memory training and it is important to understand this. What was number two? Spectacles, right?

Now, I want you to form a vivid picture in your mind of spectacles. Perhaps, it could be your own spectacles. What is important is to have a clear picture of that in your mind.

Now, I want you to think of anything but a dog. What happened? You thought of a dog. Didn't you? This shows that your mind thinks in pictures. You didn't see the word dog spelled out, you actually see a dog. Your eye is the strongest part of the memory. That is why when you see a person, you recognize their face but not recall their name.

Therefore, we remember what we see longer than what we simply hear. You should remember to actually visualize these items and form pictures.

- What was 7?
  It was Rainbow. Remember, a Rainbow with seven colours.
- What was 12?

Bananas. A dozen bananas. Visualize 12 bananas.
- What was 5?
  It is a 5 Star chocolate. Good! Get a clear picture of a 5 Star chocolate.
- What was 10?
  Ten fingers, ten toes, holding onto a ten-rupee note.
- What was 14?
  Valentine's Day. Get a good picture of two persons celebrating this day.
- What was 17?
  A magazine.
- What was 8?
  An hourglass.
- What was 11?
  A railway track.
- How about 4?
  That was a tiger with four legs.
- Do you remember 13?
  An unlucky number?
- What about 15?
  The Indian flag. Independence Day. I bet you can't forget that.
- What was 1?
  A stick. A stick is a straight line like a number one.
- What about 18?
  A voter card. Eighteen to vote for an election.
- What was 20?
  A shotgun. 20-gauge shotgun.
- What about 19?
  Potassium. Remember the 19th element of the periodic table.
- What about 16?

That's Abraham Lincoln. Abraham Lincoln was the 16th President of the United States of America.
- What was 2?
  A pair of spectacles.
- Number 6?
  Cricket
- Number 9?
  The solar system

It's time to write down this list one more time. Don't spend more than four or five minutes on it. How did you do? Better than the first time? Remember that they have to be in the correct order. What we did was an exercise in basic association. Did you get all 20? If so, great! Most people would get 15 or more. Remember that your mind remembers in pictures not words. Make an effort to actually visualize everything you are attempting to recall. Form your own pictures—the bigger, the better. This is called basic association method.

Why did we associate these objects with these numbers? Can you find logic in this? It is because there is some connection between the numbers and the objects. Once we remember all of them, we make these objects as permanent pictures in our brain. We can associate 20 new objects with these old objects in sequence. For example, we have to remember the below-mentioned objects in sequence:

1. Crow
2. Magician
3. Toothbrush
4. Statue of Liberty
5. Pressure cooker

What we will do is associate *stick* with *crow*, *spectacles* with *magician*, an *auto* with a *toothbrush*, *tiger* with the *Statue of Liberty* and *5 Star Chocolate* with a *pressure cooker*.

We will be able to get all the objects forwards and backwards; number means object and object means number.

This is how mastering memory becomes easier and easier. The brain would automatically start associating and remembering.

You will be amazed with the results as you keep learning.

FOUR

IMAGINATION METHOD

The only memory method that I knew as a child was the Acronym method. Acronym is a series of letters created using the first letter of each word. ISRO is an acronym for Indian Space Research Organisation. NATO is an acronym for North Atlantic Treaty Organization.

When I was in high school, my science teacher told me that I could learn the colours of the rainbow in the correct order by remembering the word VIBGYOR. V for Violet, I for Indigo, B for Blue, G for Green, Y for Yellow, O for Orange and R for Red.

Another acronym I learned in school was an easy way to remember the Great Lakes of USA. It is HOMES. H for Huron, O for Ontario, M for Michigan, E for Erie and S for Superior.

Can acronyms be used for everything? No. Are there more advanced ways to retain information? Yes. Every level of memory training is important, and you never know when an acronym can be used.

Do you know how a bamboo tree grows? You water it every day for five years and see nothing. In the fifth year, it will grow several feet in just a few weeks. Did it grow in a few weeks or in five years? It grew over these five years. We did not see the growth outside as the roots of the tree were growing deep. Your memory grows in the same way. Initially, you have to put in a lot of effort in learning memory techniques, but the results will be visible a few weeks later.

Acronyms and links are in this 'watering' stage. A link is a method of recalling information by telling a story. Many ancient books such as the Bible and Bhagavad Gita, Vedas and Upanishads, have been passed down through generations in this way. A link is simply connecting one thought to the next. If I ask you to memorize a list of 16 items using basic association, it will not work.

For example, number one is mountain, two is ice, three is nunber three and four is bike. What do these items have in common with the numbers?

Nothing! So, in this case, basic association will not work.

The next level is the chain of association or the link. Sit back, relax and enjoy this story. I want you to focus on seeing the images in this story vividly.

The *mountain* has *ice* on its peak and *three* trees are lined on its side. *Shah Rukh Khan* is riding a *bike* down the mountain. He has a *glass of water* in one hand and a sword in the other. At the foot of the mountain, he crashes into a *TV set* and lands on a *bed*. He bounces off the bed onto a *guitar*, and bounces off the guitar into a *ship*.

The ship arrives at *Delhi* and *Sachin Tendulkar* is waiting for him. He is wearing a *brown hat* and *black boots*. He hands him a *cheque worth ₹1,00,000* and the *keys* to a brand new *BMW car*. Shah Rukh Khan drives his BMW back to the mountain.

Now, we are going to do this one more time. The difference is that I now want you to repeat the items out aloud. By the way, if you move your hands and enact the events, you will be able to etch the pictures in your mind. Let us begin.

Mountain has ice on its peak and three trees are lined on its side. Shah Rukh Khan is riding a bike down the mountain. He has a glass of water in one hand and a sword in the other.

Repeat: He has a glass of water in one hand and a sword in the other. At the bottom of the mountain, he crashes into a TV set.

Repeat: At the bottom of the mountain, he crashes into a TV set. He lands on a bed and bounces off it onto a guitar. He then bounces off the guitar onto a ship.

Repeat: He lands on a bed and bounces off it onto a guitar. He then bounces off the guitar and into a ship. The ship arrives in Delhi and Mr Sachin Tendulkar is waiting for him.

Repeat: The ship arrives in Delhi and Mr Sachin Tendulkar is waiting for him. He is wearing a brown hat and black boots.

Repeat: He is wearing a brown hat and black boots. He hands him a cheque worth ₹1,00,000 and the keys to a BMW car.

Repeat: He hands him a cheque for ₹1,00,000 and the keys to a brand new BMW car. Shah Rukh Khan then drives the BMW car back to the mountain.

Repeat: He then drives the BMW car back to the mountain.

Did you enact the incidents? I always do. I hold out my hands as if I am holding a glass of water and a sword. I will bounce like I'm on the guitar and act like I am Sachin Tendulkar, and I stick out my hands like they have a cheque worth ₹1,00,000 in them.

Let's do this one more time. Here we go. Focus on the story: The mountain has ice on its peak and three trees are lined on its side.

Repeat: The mountain has ice on its peak and trees are lined on its side. Shah Rukh Khan is riding a bike down the mountain.

Repeat: Shah Rukh Khan is riding a bike down the mountain. He has a glass of water in one hand and a sword in the other.

Repeat: He has a glass of water in one hand and a sword in the other. At the foot of the mountain, he crashes into a TV set.

Repeat: At the foot of the mountain, he crashes into a TV set. He lands on a bed, bounces off it onto a guitar, and bounces off the guitar into a ship.

Repeat: He lands on a bed, bounces off onto a guitar, and bounces off the guitar onto a ship. The ship arrives at Delhi and Sachin Tendulkar is waiting for him.

Repeat: The ship arrives in Delhi and Sachin Tendulkar is waiting for him. He is wearing a brown hat and black boots. Say it again; he is wearing a brown hat and black boots. He hands him over a cheque worth ₹1,00,000 and the keys to a brand new BMW car.

Repeat: He hands him over a cheque for ₹1,00,000 and the keys to a brand new BMW car. He then drives the car back to mountain. Say it again; he then drives the car back to mountain.

Now, it is time to see how many you recalled. Write down all the items on a sheet of paper. Don't write out the story; instead, simply write the items in the story. For example, *mountain* will be the first item on the list.

Set the book aside now and write the items down. There should be 16 items. Do not spend more than four to five minutes on this exercise. After you are done, come back and check your answers below.

Answers

1. Mountain
2. Bike
3. Shah Rukh Khan
4. Glass of water
5. Sword
6. TV set
7. Bed
8. Guitar
9. Ship
10. Delhi

11. Sachin Tendulkar
12. Brown hat
13. Black boots
14. Cheque for ₹1,00,000
15. Keys
16. BMW car

How to Use Effectively Imagination

When you create an image or story to remember a word/object, keep in mind the following points to make the picture more memorable.

- Use positive and pleasant images. The brain often blocks out unpleasant ones.
- Exaggerate the size of important parts of the image.
- Use humour! Funny, illogical and peculiar things are easier to remember than serious, logical and normal ones.
- Similarly, rude or sexual images are difficult to forget.
- Use symbols like red traffic lights, pointing fingers, etc.
- Use all the senses to code information or dress up an image. Remember that your image can contain sounds, smells, tastes, touch, movements and feelings.
- Vivid and colourful images are easier to remember than drab ones.
- When conjuring up these images, give each item a distinct background. This aids in recalling the items separately and helps avoiding confusion.
- Use three-dimensional images and movements. They make the image more vivid. Movement can be used either to maintain the flow of association or can help to remember actions.

The important thing is that you should be able to relate the object clearly to what you want to remember. It should also be vivid enough so that you are able to recall it whenever you want.

Now that you have memorized 16 objects through imagination, can you also build your imagination to remember the 23 objects mentioned below? Try to keep your imagination as animated as possible.

mobile, cupboard, book, television, glass, dog, refrigerator, bus, helmet, wallpaper, leaves, sweater, suitcase, cake, lemon, bicycle, handkerchief, coffee, seminar, tape recorder, switchboard, window, sugar

FIVE

LOCATION METHOD (OR METHOD OF LOCI)

In 477 BC, a Greek poet, Simonides, amazed everyone with a display of his sharp memory. He was attending a banquet when the roof of the building collapsed and killed many attendants. The bodies which were crushed beyond recognition, had to be identified. Simonides came to the rescue by recalling the names of every person in that building and where they were sitting. He claimed that he did this by imagining the people where they sat at the table during the banquet. This method of recalling information in this manner is called the Method of Loci (*loci* being Latin for 'places').

The ancients remembered things by imagining that they were taking a walk on a familiar path and placing things to be remembered at various places along the way. This method works because it organizes the material to be remembered and it encourages elaborate processing and memorable imagery.

Ancient orators used this technique to remember speeches, as it combines the use of organization, visual memory and association. Before using this technique, you must identify a path that you have already taken. This can be the walk from your bedroom to your classroom, a walk around your house—anything that is familiar. What is essential is that you have a vivid visual memory of the path and objects along it. Once you have determined your path, you should imagine taking a walk and identifying specific landmarks as you pass them. For example, the first landmark on the way to your campus could be your bedroom; the next may be the front of the residence hall, then a familiar statue, etc. The number of landmarks you choose will depend on the number of things you want to remember.

Once you have visualized the landmarks, you are ready to use the path to remember the objects/information. Do this by mentally associating each piece of information that you need to remember with one of these landmarks. For example, if you are trying to remember a list of mnemonics, you might remember the first acronyms by picturing a SCUBA gear in your dorm room (SCUBA is an acronym).

You do not have to limit this to a path. You can use the same type of technique with just about any visual image that you can divide into specific sections. The most important thing is that you should use something that is very familiar.

 Exercise

- If someone reads a list of unrelated words to you, just once, how many do you think you could remember? Give it a try. Have someone read a list of 10 words to you at a slow but steady pace (about one word per second). Rather than using any of the memory techniques presented here, simply try to concentrate on the words and remember them. How many words did you remember?
- Now take a few minutes to identify a path or object that you can use in the method of loci. Familiarize yourself with each section in your path or object. Go through each of the loci (locations) and visualize them as best as you can. Remember, it is important to be able to visualize and recall each location

readily. Once you have done this, have your friend read you a different list of words. This time, try to create visual images of the words associated with the locations.

This may not be easy at first, but with practice, you should be able to create these visual images more easily. If it is difficult for you to form these images quickly, practise on some more lists of objects until you have improved. Chances are, when you get used to this technique, you will be able to remember more words.

Let us take an example:

Choose from the following 10 locations in your school or college. These locations should be permanent and you should be able to recall them automatically. For example:

School bus parking area, entrance gate, security guard, assembly ground, staircase, Principal's cabin, staffroom, washroom, classroom door, bench

Now, you have these 10 objects to remember:

Globe, banana, camel, Titanic, pillow, APJ Abdul Kalam, diamonds, Sri Lanka, stadium, bracelet

How to memorize:
Place one object in one location and associate that object with the location vividly.

For example, in the *school bus parking area*, several *globes* are placed.

In front of the *entrance gate*, *bananas* are hanging.

The *security guard* is riding a *camel*.

The school's *assembly ground* is on the *Titanic*.

The *staircase* is full of colourful *pillows*.
In the *Principal's cabin*, *Dr APJ Abdul Kalam* is seated.
The *staffroom* is stacked with *diamonds*.
The *washroom* is in *Sri Lanka*.
The *classroom door* opens onto a huge *stadium*.
On the *bench*, you find a golden *bracelet*.

Once you associate these objects with the locations, you will be able to recall all of them quickly without missing a single object.

SIX

ANCIENT MEMORY METHODS

The sages and yogis of our country were known to possess great control over their mind and were able to perform amazing feats as a result of that. The path to mind control is through deep concentration and meditation. If you want to harness the energies of our mind, you have to practise meditation. The world has awakened to this fact and more and more people are taking to meditation to keep the body as well as mind in a healthy state. When you have a healthy mind, you have a healthy memory.

During olden times, there were no devices, equipments or books to store and transfer knowledge from. Slowly, books came into being and other technical tools followed to help in this regard.

Radio entertained us over the years, especially during its golden era between 1970s and 1980s. I am a huge cricket fan. As a teenager, I remember listening to the cricket commentary on the radio. I can also remember the pictures I created in my head to visualize the cricket match, the players and the crowd.

Imagine a lemon sitting on the table in front of you. It is the size of a grapefruit. Take your right hand and visualize yourself cutting the lemon in half. Do you see the juices flowing on the tablecloth? Sitting on the table are the two halves of the lemon. Pick up one of the lemon halves and hold it up to your nose. Do you get the fresh smell of the lemon? Now, holding the lemon against your mouth, squeeze it and let the juices drip down your throat.

Did you salivate? Did your face squish up into an expression that shows that you have actually bitten into something sour? Why did you make those expressions? What provoked them? Your mind thinks in pictures and often, it cannot tell the difference between an actual or mental picture. Sportsmen visualize a lot of their actions on the field—golf swings, batting swings or catching footballs—long before they actually do those things. If the visualization is strong enough, then you are conditioning your mind for success.

Here is a modern day example. Most of us use computers in some fashion. When you have information you wish to keep, what do you do? You store it on a disk, a CD, print it and file it.

Let us say a hacker got into your computer and deleted all the files, directories and program titles. Although everything is still in your computer hard drive, it is not labeled. The information would still be there, but finding it would be a problem. The analogy is this: Everything you have ever seen, heard or done is still in your memory. Accessing and retrieving it is what is difficult.

Hence you save all the information in the computer by separating them into files, naming them and putting them in a folder. The retrieval becomes easy. Similarly, the books in the library are stored systematically classified on the basis of their authors. That is why it is easy for a librarian to get a book for you.

Our brain works in a similar manner. Whatever we see, hear, read, experience, say, do, write, gets stored in our brain. The problem is that they may be stored haphazardly. Hence, when you need to retrieve some information, you are aware that you know it, but you are unable to recall the information at that instant.

Therefore, systematic storage of information in the brain is very essential for quick retrieval. In this direction, the system developed by the Romans, allows you to create files and directories in your mind and store information in those files. The Romans discovered that you need five things to recall anything: numbers, poems, scriptures, dates, presentations or names. The items are the same that your computer uses: focus, location, code, action and review.

Here are some questions about the town that you live in. Can you visualize the school? What about the fire department, your home, the police station, the public swimming pool, the river, the park, the hotel, the car dealership or restaurant? Can you visualize all of them? These are what the Romans would call files.

The Romans started at the north end of their town and then chose an item like a park, river, stadium, tree or an object that stood out, and that would be their first file. As they moved south through the town, they would choose items in a very systematic north to south method until they had may be 25 or 30 files.

What you need to do is visualize your town from a bird's eye view. The top of the page is the North; pick ten items that you can use as files. Remember, good files are buildings, restaurants, schools, houses or petrol bunks. Work north to south or east to west, or even clockwise, to make it logical.

Once again, pick ten files in your city; write them down and memorize them. How did you do? Did you zip through it? Now, you have just created your first ten files. I am going to give you ten pictures and you are going to file them as ten city files.

First, let me ask you a few questions. Can you remember every time you have gotten into a car and driven to some place? No? But I bet you can tell me the time when your car collided with someone else's. You could probably tell me the time of the day, location and what car you were driving. That picture was vivid and it had emotions tied to it. I bet you do not remember all the times you went to a movie or had dinner with someone, but you remember your first date or break up. These things have emotions tied to them and remain in your memory.

The first step is to select a familiar route in your city and fix few locations that are known to you. These will act as files. You need to drive these city files into your memory and know them forwards and backwards. Below you will find a list of ten words. Use the city files you have created to place each of these objects mentally at your location and visualize it alongside an action.

If the first word you memorize is water then visualize a giant glass of water. Remember the more vivid and larger than life your image is, the better will your ability be to recall it. Scan through the list as quickly as possible, use your locations in your city files and imagine larger than life images:

1. Photo album
2. Alkaa
3. Horizon
4. Hurricane
5. Call Funny
6. The colour red
7. Connection
8. Delhiwala
9. Floor
10. George Washington

Now write down the ten pictures to test your ability to recall these words. Do not write down the file or action, just visualize it. Do not get stuck on any one item; you can always come back to it. You should ask yourself what the file was, and you will be able to retrieve the picture. How did you fare? Did you score a ten?

First, make a note of ten states of the United States of America in alphabetical order:

1. Alabama
2. Alaska
3. Arizona
4. Arkansas
5. California
6. Colorado
7. Connecticut
8. Delaware
9. Florida
10. Georgia

How many did you get right? If you got nine or ten, pat yourself on the back. If you got eight or less, it could be because either you did not know your file, or your picture was not vivid enough. Make sure that you know your files by heart and that the pictures created are vivid. We turned ten abstract words into pictures and attached them to our files. Would you believe me if I just told you that I learned the first ten states of the United States in alphabetical order? Let's see how this was done.

1. *photo album.* The first state is *Alabama.* A *photo album* for *Alabama.*
2. *Alkaa.* Name of a girl sounds like *Alaska.*
3. *Horizon.* It sounds like *Arizona.*
4. *Hurricane.* Almost too easy. *Arkansas.*
5. Call *Funny.* Rhyming like *California.*
6. The *colour red. Colorado*?
7. *connection.* Easily we can recall...*Connecticut.*
8. *Delhiwala.* Sounds like *Delaware.*
9. *Floor. Floor* and *Florida,* you can recall easily.
10. *George.* How about *Georgia*?

Did you think it was going to be that easy? You have learned quite a bit in this chapter.

What has been done here is since you did not have a readymade or proper image of these states in your mind, you tried to put some sense into nonsensical words to build a connection that gives a substitution effect or some meaning close to the actual word. Thereafter, you have associated this picture of the state with the fixed files that you have already made.

Next time, when you recall the file, you remember the matching word. That leads you to the actual word or term. Thereby, this will work as a prompt to recall the actual word. Hence this is 70 per cent to 80 per cent better than rote memory, which a majority of students follow these days.

Try and memorize all the states of the USA:

Alabama, Alaska, Arizona, Aransas, California, Colorado, Connecticut, Delaware, Florida, George, Hawaii, Idaho, Illinois, Indiana, Iowa, Kansas, Kentucky, Louisiana, Maine, Maryland, Massachusetts, Michigan, Minnesota, Mississippi, Missouri, Montana, Nebraska, Nevada, New Hampshire, New Jersey, New Mexico, New York, North Carolina, North Dakota, Ohio, Oklahoma, Oregon, Pennsylvania, Rhode Island, South Carolina, South Dakota, Tennessee, Texas, Utah, Vermont, Virginia, Washington, West Virginia, Wisconsin, Wyoming

We have already learnt 10 states. Now associate the other 40 states with the images:

Hawaii	–	*Hawaa*
Idaho	–	Idiot
Illinois	–	Iliana

Indiana	–	India
Iowa	–	Ayyo
Kansas	–	Kansa (Uncle of Lord Krishna)
Kentucky	–	KFC Chicken
Louisiana	–	Loose
Maine	–	*Maine Pyar Kiya* (Hindi film)
Mary Land	–	Mary Land
Massachusetts	–	Mask, Chest
Michigan	–	Michael Jackson
Minnesota	–	Minor
Mississippi	–	Miss (Madam)
Missouri	–	Mysore
Montana	–	Mountain
Nebraska	–	New Bracket
Nevada	–	Never
New Hampshire	–	New Hump Shahar
New Jersey	–	New Jersey
New Mexico	–	New Mixi
New York	–	New year
North Carolina	–	North car
North Dakota	–	North Dakota (Name of Indian Air Force Plane)
Ohio	–	Ayyo
Oklahoma	–	Akele (Home-Alone)—Home
Oregon	–	Orange
Pennsylvania	–	Pen–Veena
Rhode Island	–	Jonty Rhodes or rod
South Carolina	–	South car

South Dakota	–	South Daaku (Hindi it means—Decoit)
Tennessee	–	Tennis
Texas	–	Textbook
Utah	–	Utter
Vermont	–	Permanent
Virginia	–	Virgin
Washington	–	Washing one ton
West Virginia	–	West Virgin
Wisconsin	–	Wise Cousin
Wyoming	–	Why I am wrong

Now, we have memorized all the 50 states of the USA. What a great achievement!

 **Exercise**

Can you memorize the following?

1. Washing Machine
2. A dam
3. Chef cooking the sun
4. Medicine
5. Man in a rowboat
6. A dam and cue balls
7. Carjack
8. Van burning
9. Hair
10. Tie
11. Polka dots
12. Tailor

13. Filling up one more glass
14. Piece
15. Blue cannon or Bachchan
16. Beard
17. Ants drawing
18. College grant
19. Fog, mist or haze
20. Garfield, the cat
21. Author
22. City of Cleveland
23. Benji, the Walt Disney Dog
24. City of Cleveland (Cleveland had become president twice)
25. Mount McKinnely (in Alaska)
26. Roses
27. Raft
28. Wilson tennis ball
29. Hard surface
30. Cooler
31. Vacuum cleaner
32. Roses
33. Man telling truth
34. Eyeball
35. Ken doll (Barbie and Barbie)
36. Airplane 'landing'
37. Gate with water rushing through it
38. Ford truck
39. Peanut butter
40. Jelly beans
41. Bushes
42. Lint
43. Bushes
44. Bahamas

45. Triumph

There you have it. Now, number 1–45 and see how many words you can recall. Remember that not all the words will come to mind right away; skip whatever you cannot recall and continue. Do not get slowed down with the ones that you do not recall. Finish the ones that you do know and then return to the ones that you initially missed.

So, what did we just memorize? Well, we were talking about names; so if you guessed 45 names, you are correct! But, let's take it one step further; these are important names! They are the names of the 45 Presidents of The United States!

Here are the answers:

1.	Washing Machine	–	Washington
2.	A dam	–	Adams
3.	Chef cooking the sun	–	Jefferson (Chef sun)
4.	Medicine	–	Madison
5.	Man in a rowboat	–	Monroe
6.	A dam and cue balls	–	Q. Adams
7.	Carjack	–	Jackson
8.	Van burning	–	Van Buren
9.	Hair	–	Harrison
10.	Tie	–	Tyler
11.	Polka dots	–	Polk
12.	Tailor	–	Taylor
13.	Filling up one more glass	–	Fillmore
14.	Piece	–	Pierce
15.	Blue cannon (Bachchan)	–	Buchanan
16.	Beard	–	Abe Lincoln

17. Ants drawing – Andrew (Johnson)
18. College grant – Grant
19. Fog, mist or haze – Hayes
20. Garfield the cat – Garfield
21. Author – Arthur
22. City of Cleveland – Cleveland
23. Benji, the Walt Disney dog – Benjamin (Harrison)
24. City of Cleveland – Cleveland
25. Mount McKinley (in Alaska) – McKinley
26. Roses – Roosevelt
27. Raft – Taft
28. Wilson tennis ball – Wilson
29. Hard surface – Harding
30. Cooler – Coolidge
31. Vacuum cleaner – Hoover
32. Roses – Franklin Roosevelt
33. Man telling truth – Truman
34. Eyeball – Eisenhower
35. Ken doll (Barbie and Ken) – Kennedy
36. Airplane landing – Lyndon Johnson
37. Gate with water rushing through it – Nixon (Watergate)
38. Ford truck – Ford
39. Peanut butter – Jimmy Carter
40. Jelly Beans – Reagan
41. Bushes – Bush
42. Lint – Clinton

Ancient Memory Methods • 41

43. Bushes	–	Bush
44. Bahamas	–	Obama
45. Triumph	–	Donald Trump

I am sure you now remember the names of 45 Presidents of the United States of America. What a superb job!

 Exercise II

Turn the following names into pictures:

Frank
Harold
Tommy
George
Blaine
Sally
Sarah
Natalie
Daniel
Rebecca
Heidi
Judy
Melissa
Missy
William
Davey
Barney
Jacob

Burt

Look at the pictures below:

Frank	–	Franky
Harold	–	Hair-old
Tommy	–	Tom & Jerry
George	–	George
Blaine	–	Blown
Sally	–	Sail
Sarah	–	Saree
Natalie	–	Nut-Ali
Daniel	–	Don
Rebecca	–	Roebuck Shoes
Heidi	–	Hide
Judy	–	Judo
Melissa	–	Mails
Missy	–	Miss
William	–	Wills
Davey	–	Devil
Barney	–	Born
Jacob	–	Jackal
Burt	–	But

If you are not comfortable or unfamiliar with any of the above images, you may change them with what you know in your language, subject or what you can relate with something personal to you. You will be able to recall all these words automatically.

Exercise III

Let us now try to remember the list of 29 words below:

Aruna
Charminar
Tea
Lalu Prasad Yadav
Beach
Mahatma Gandhi
Hari Anna
Hima
Apple
Music
Bhopal
Coconut
Sachin Tendulkar
Money
Megh
Maize-Ram
Naagin
Harbhajan Singh
Sick
Oh-Rickshaw
Desert
Dehradun
Taj Mahal
Rajinikanth
Tripura Sundari

Bay of Bengal
M.S. Dhoni
Chitti Garh
Laddu (Tirupati Laddu)

If you have memorized all of them, you will be surprised to see that you have indeed memorized the names of 29 states of India.

Aruna	–	Arunachal Pradesh
Charminar	–	Telangana
Tea	–	Assam
Lalu Prasad Yadav	–	Bihar
Beach	–	Goa
Mahatma Gandhi	–	Gujarat
Hari Anna	–	Haryana
Hima	–	Himachal Pradesh
Apple	–	Jammu & Kashmir
Music	–	Karnataka
Bhopal	–	Madhya Pradesh
Coconut	–	Kerala
Sachin Tendulkar	–	Maharashtra
Money	–	Manipur
Megh	–	Meghalaya
Maize-Ram	–	Mizoram
Naagin	–	Nagaland
Harbhajan Singh	–	Punjab
Sick	–	Sikkim
Oh-Rickshaw	–	Odisha
Desert	–	Rajasthan

Ancient Memory Methods • 45

Dehradun	–	Uttarakhand
Tajmahal	–	Uttar Pradesh
Rajinikanth	–	Tamil Nadu
Tripura Sundari	–	Tripura
Bay of Bengal	–	West Bengal
M.S. Dhoni	–	Jharkhand
Chitti Garh	–	Chhattisgarh
Laddu (Tirupati Laddu)	–	Andhra Pradesh

You are supposed to memorize all of them by visualizing a story connecting one word to the other.

Imagine:

A girl named *Aruna* (*Arunachal Pradesh*) went to see *Charminar* (*Telangana*). She went to have a cup of *tea* (*Assam*), where Mr *Lalu Prasad Yadav* (*Bihar*) was selling *tea*. They went to a *beach* (*Goa*). They saw *Mahatma Gandhi* (*Gujarat*) there. He was shouting *Hari Anna* (*Haryana*). A girl named *Hima* (*Himachal Pradesh*) gave an *apple* (*Jammu & Kashmir*) to *Mahatma Gandhi*. After eating it, he began to play *music* (*Carnatic music—Karnataka*). He went to *Bhopal* (*Madhya Pradesh*). In *Bhopal*, people gave him a *coconut* (*Kerala*). Mahatma Gandhi gave the coconut to *Sachin Tendulkar* (*Maharashtra*). *Sachin* gave him some *money* (*Manipur*) in return. In the sky, there is thick *megh* (*Meghalaya*). From the *megh*, filled with *maize, Lord Ram* emerged (*Maize-Ram—Mizoram*). A *naagin* (*Nagaland*) danced in front of him. It stung *Harbhajan Singh* (*Punjab*). He fell *sick* (*Sikkim*). He shouted, '*Oh Rickshaw!*' (*Orissa/Odisha*) and the rickshaw fellow went through a *desert* (*Rajasthan*) to *Dehradun* (*Uttarakhand*). In *Dehradun*, he saw the *Taj Mahal* (Uttar Pradesh) built in white marble and the superstar *Rajinikanth* (Tamil Nadu) was dancing in front of it. Next to him was actor *Tripura Sundari* (Tripura). Both of them slipped and fell into the *Bay of Bengal* (*West Bengal*). Former Indian cricket captain *M.S. Dhoni* (Jharkhand) dived into the sea and brought them to *Chitti Garh* (*Chattisgarh*), where he treated them with a *laddu* (*Tirupati Laddu—Andhra Pradesh*).

I am sure you now remember all the 29 states of India.

One question that arises is how you could know Mahatma Gandhi means Gujarat. It is common sense. In school, you are taught about the peculiarities of a particular state which include people, monuments, companies, the crops grown there, temples, zoos or anything that stands out in relation to that state. Since you already know them, you may change them suiting your requirement and build a story.

You may be able to remember all the states without the story, but you may miss a couple. You will get all the 29 states right with this method and it is fun to learn. It stays with you for a long time.

Now, keep the book away and teach this story to your mother, father, brother or friend and you will be surprised at how they are able to recall all the 29 states instantly. That is the power of this technique.

Here is another exercise:

Raju
Raadha
Jockey
Gira diya
Fakir
Neelam
Jail
Venkata Ramana
Shankara-Daya

Narayana
Kalam
Prathibha
Mukherjee
Rameshwaram-Govinda

If you have memorized these 14 words, it means, you have memorized all the 14 presidents of India.

Raju	–	Dr Rajendra Prasad
Raadha	–	Dr S. Radhakrishnan
Jockey	–	Dr Zakir Hussain
Gira diya	–	V.V. Giri
Fakir	–	Dr Fakhruddin Ali Ahmed
Neelam	–	Neelam Sanjiva Reddy
Jail	–	Giani Zail Singh
Venkata Ramana	–	R. Venkataraman
Shankara-Daya	–	Dr Shankar Dayal Sharma
Narayana	–	K. R. Narayanan
Kalam	–	Dr A.P.J. Abdul Kalam
Pratibha	–	Pratibha Patil
Mukherjee	–	Dr Pranab Mukerjee
Rameshwaram-Govinda	–	Ram Nath Kovind

I am sure you have become an expert in storytelling by now.

If it is still vague, imagine this...

Raju (*Dr Rajendra Prasad*) fell in love with a girl named *Radha* (*Dr Radhakrishnan*). They were riding a horse like *jockeys* (*Dr Zakir Hussain*). The horse *gira diya* (*V.V. Giri*), the Hindi phrase for 'drop'. A *Fakir* (*Dr Fakhruddin Ali Ahmed*) had a *neelam* (Blue Sapphire—*Neelam Sanjiva Reddy*). Some people caught them and put them in *jail* (*Zail Singh*). They were worshipping *Venkata Ramana* (*R. Venkataraman*), but he did not appear. They began to pray to *Lord Shankara* to show some *daya* (*Dr Shankar Dayal Sharma*), Hindi word for 'mercy'. But, he did not appear. Finally, Lord *Narayana* (*K.R. Narayanan*) appeared and gave them a *kalam* (*Dr A.P.J. Abdul Kalam*), Hindi for 'pen'. Raju and Radha did not have *prathiba* (*Prathibha Patil*), Hindi for 'talent', and hence, they went to *Pranab Mukerjee* (*Dr Pranab Mukerjee*) for help. He said, he was retiring, and sent them to *Rameshwaram* and reciting *Govinda–Govinda* (*Ram Nath Kovind*).

This is how we can make a story. You can make whatever changes you feel like. What you need to learn here is the idea.

SEVEN

SUBSTITUTION METHOD

Sometimes, you are unable to visualize a picture in place of terms or words you come across. That is where the substitution technique comes handy. This is like putting some sense into what you want to remember, which helps the brain to imagine something different.

Whenever you come across a new word or sentence, you can substitute it by another word or sentence you already know. This is called the Substitution Method. There are many applications of this method and you are going to learn them in this chapter.

(a) Look at the examples given below as to how we can visualize these words:

Carbon	–	Car full of buns
Hydrogen	–	High dragon
Beryllium	–	Bury him
Nitrogen	–	Night-rose-gin
Oxygen	–	Ox-zen car
Fluorine	–	Floor-rin soap
Phosphorous	–	Prosperous
Titanium	–	Tighten him

Try the following words:
Selenium

Bismuth
Gadolinium
Armstrong
Hysteresis

(b) Let us look at the following scientific words:

Phaseolus Aureus (Green Gram or moong)	–	Faceless-Arushi
Pennisetum Glaucum (bajra)	–	Pen-set-Typhoid
Sorghum Vulgare (jowar)	–	Swaragam-vulgar
Gossypium herbaceum (cotton)	–	Gossip-herbal
Hippocampus (hippopotamus)	–	Campus
Musa Paradisiaca (banana)	–	Mousi-paradise
Oryza Sativa (rice)	–	Oridha-Saturday
Canis familiaris (dog)	–	Canal-family
Capra hircus (Goat)	–	Cap-circus
Equus caballus (Horse)	–	Eq-cab
Corpus Callosum	–	car-push-call-someone

(c) Other complicated long words:

Floccinaucinihilipilification – Flask-nose-hell-Philip-occasion
Supercalifragilisticexpialidocious – Super-qualis-frog-lipstick-expired-doses
Pneumonoultramicroscopicsilicovolcanoconiosis – Human-ultimate-microscope-silk-volcano-cone of ash

If you can use the above method skilfully, you will be able to remember all kinds of scientific or technical words, names of medicines, botanical names and terms related to accountancy and engineering, etc. You will also be able to remember the elements of the Periodic Table. Make a list of all the elements, substitute them with words and see if you can remember.

(d) Let us try to remember the electrochemical series:

1.	Antimony-Aunty	–	Mona
2.	Arsenic	–	Arsenal
3.	Iron	–	vessel
4.	Cadmium	–	Cat-mew
5.	Zinc	–	Sink
6.	Copper	–	Cup-upper
7.	Gold	–	Necklace
8.	Silver	–	Anklets
9.	Molybdenum	–	Moulded bed
10.	Tin	–	Thin
11.	Lead	–	Laddu
12.	Aluminium	–	Alu-Mini
13.	Mercury	–	Mary-cure
14.	Manganese	–	Mango
15.	Platinum	–	Plate
16.	Palladium	–	Pallu
17.	Cobalt	–	Cobra-belt
18.	Nickel	–	Nikaalo
19.	Bismuth	–	Biscuit

Having done the substitution, visualize a story using all the words.

One day, *Aunty* Mona (*Antimony*) told you that she wanted to store some *Arsenal*. You told her to store the weapons in an iron vessel. As she was keeping them, a cat came and *mewed* (*Cadmium*). She got frightened and fell into the *sink* (*Zinc*). You used a *cup* to bring Aunty to the *upper* (*Copper*) surface. You gave her a *necklace* (*Gold*), *anklets* (*Silver*) and made her sleep on the *moulded bed* (*Molybdenum*). As she slept on the bed, she began to grow *thin* (*Tin*). You gave her a *laddu* (*Lead*) to eat, but Aunty wanted *alu (potato)*, which was *mini* (*Aluminium*) in size. You called for Dr *Mary* to *cure* (*Mercury*) your Aunty. On her way, Dr Mary bought a *mango* (*Manganese*), kept it on a *plate* (*Platinum*), covered it with a saree's *pallu* (*Palladium*), brought a *cobra* and tied it as a *belt* (*Cobalt*) around her own waist. Unable to breathe, Aunty was crying *nikalo! nikalo!* (*Nickel*), Hindi word for 'get it out'. You got rid of the cobra and gave Aunty a *biscuit* (*Bismuth*) to eat and she was fine thereafter.

The moment you remember this story, you will be able to recollect all the 19 elements of electrochemical series.

(e) Can you remember the structure of a typical cell?

1. Cell wall	–	Cell company waale
2. Cell Membrane	–	Cell Membership
3. Protoplasm	–	Photo
4. Cytoplasm	–	Site
5. Nucleoplasm	–	Necklace
6. Mitochondria	–	Mitha-candy
7. Golgi bodies	–	Gale-body
8. Endoplasmic reticulum	–	End return
9. Ribosome	–	Ribbon
10. Lysosome	–	Lies
11. Centrosome	–	Centre
12. Plastid	–	Plaster
13. Vacuole	–	Vacuum cleaner
14. Nucleus	–	New

The substitution pictures are given. Can you visualize these words in a story form and remember the structure of a typical cell?

(f) Let us see as to how we can remember forms of electromagnetic radiation.

Radio Waves
Microwaves
Infrared
Visible light
Ultra Violet
X-rays
Gamma Rays
Cosmic Rays

Make up a story that you were listening to *radio*, went into the kitchen and saw the *microwave*, which was *red* in colour. It was *visible*. Suddenly, it became *violet*. As you wondered what just happened, it began to emit *X-rays* and these rays began to hit you. You went to Dr *Gamma* and he asked you to go to the *cosmic* world for treatment.

If you can visualize this story, you will be able to recall all the types of electromagnetic radiation.

(g) Can you memorize one of the longest place names in the world? It is the name of a hill in New Zealand named Taumata whakatangi hangakoauau o tamatea turi pukakapiki maunga horo nuku pokai whenua kitanatahu.

We have to break this using the substitution method: Tomato-White angi-hang-cow out-angi-hang-cow out-tomato-tea-uru-rip-kaka-piki-mounanga-horn-kuppa-Kuwait-kit-natak

Once you have made the story up, it will become easy for you to remember and recall longest place names in the world.

(h) Let us recollect the Spanish name of Los Angeles:

El Pueblo de Nuestra Señora la Reina de los Ángeles

Substitute the above with the words you know: Lee-pebble-die-news-tree-scene-raallu-raina-die-Los-Anjali-loss-die-Puri-Seenu-cool. You will be able remember the full name of Los Angeles.

(i) Now using the same method, can you memorize countries and capitals?

In school or a college, they only tell you to learn things by repeating after the teacher. But the limitation with the repetition method is that it is difficult and soon you forget what you learnt. Hence, you need to use the following method.

Countries and capitals:

Hungary	–	Budapest (Hungry—Buddha eating paste)
Bulgaria	–	Sofia (Bull *gir gaya*—sofa)
Iran	–	Tehran (I ran-*tu* ran)
Argentina	–	Buenos Aires (Urgent-Tina—Blue saree)
Bahamas	–	Nassau (Brahmin—Nasa)
Dominica	–	Roseau (Dominos Pizza—Rose)
Philippines	–	Manila (Philips TV—Money laa)

The method that was followed here included substituting the names of the countries and capitals with the words that you knew and associated them with. Using this method, you can try to memorize all the countries and their capitals.

(j) Memorizing English vocabulary: You can also use this method for memorizing English vocabulary. Say for instance, you have come across a new word—abase. The method that we follow is to first look into the dictionary and find out the meaning of the word. The meaning of this word is to behave in a way that belittles or degrades (someone). However, you might soon forget the meaning you just looked up, because it is just a one-step process—the word and meaning association.

To remember the meaning for a long time, you need to follow a three-step process:

Step 1
New word: Abase.
Find out the meaning from the dictionary and understand it: Behave in a way that belittles or degrades (someone).

Step 2
Find out if you know any part of this new word, 'abase'.

You do—'base', meaning the lowest part or edge of something, especially the part on which it rests or is supported.

Step 3
Associate what you know to what you do not. In the sense, I know, 'base' means the lowest part of something, and what I do not know is 'abase' means to behave in a way that belittles or degrades.

Once you understand these three steps, every time you come across 'abase', you will automatically remember 'base'. 'Base' means the lowest part or edge of something, which will lead you to 'abase' which means 'to behave in a way that belittles or degrades. This is how the memory becomes permanent in the brain.

Next word: Acclimatize—become accustomed to a new climate or new conditions; adjust

Step 1: Look up the meaning.

Step 2: You know 'climate' in 'acclimatize'.
Step 3: Associate 'climate' with 'adjusting'.
You will not forget it. You'll need to acclimatize yourself back to regular life again.

Next word: Aegis—protection, backing, or support of a particular person or organization
Step 1: Look up the meaning.
Step 2: You know 'age' in 'aegis'.
Step 3: Associate 'age' with 'protection'. Young and old people need protection.

Next Word: Affront—an action or remark that causes outrage or offence
Step 1: Look up the meaning.
Step 2: You know 'front' in 'affront'.
Step 3: Associate 'front' with 'offence'. In front of others, do not offend anyone.

Next word: Appall—greatly dismay or horrify
Step 1: Look up the meaning.
Step 2: you know 'apple' in 'appall'.
Step 3: Associate 'apple' with 'horrify'. When you asked for the rate of an apple, you were horrified at the exorbitant price quoted by the fruit seller.

Next word: Baleful—threatening harm; menacing
Step 1: Look up the meaning.
Step 2: You know bhelpuri, bails, bail in 'baleful'.
Step 3: Associate 'bhelpuri' with 'menacing'. Eating bhelpuris on the roadside can be menacing for the stomach. Or, when the bails fall off (in cricket), it is threatening for the team. Or, menacing criminals cannot not be bailed out of jail.

Next Word: Bellicose—demonstrating aggression and willingness to fight
Step 1: Look up the meaning.
Step 2: You know 'belly' in 'bellicose'.
Step 3: Associate 'belly' with 'aggression'. The man with a big belly showed aggression.

Next word: Blight—a thing that spoils or damages something
Step 1: Look up the meaning.
Step 2: You know 'light' in 'blight'.
Step 3: Associate 'light' with 'spoil'. When lightning strikes, all the electrical equipment in the house might get spoiled.

Next word: Bluster—talk in a loud, aggressive, or indignant way with little effect
Step 1: Look up the meaning.
Step 2: You know 'blast' in 'bluster'.
Step 3: Associate 'blast' with 'loud'. Their unconvincing fights sounded like blasts loud enough to wake up the neighbours.

Next word: Certitude—absolute certainty or conviction that something is the case
Step 1: Look up the meaning.
Step 2: You know 'certificate, certify or certain' in 'certitude'.
Step 3: Associate 'certificate' with 'certainty'. When a certificate provides the absolute certainty that you have passed an examination. Or, my message ascertains that I will meet you tomorrow.

Next word: Careen—(of a ship) tilt; lean over
Step 1: Look up the meaning.
Step 2: You know Kareena Kapoor in 'careen'.
Step 3: Associate 'Kareena Kapoor' with 'tilt'. The ship in which Kareena Kapoor was sailing tilted on both sides from time to time.

The basic idea is to have as much base memory as possible. You can form your base memory by reading lots of books, visiting places, participating in seminars, meeting people, through the Internet, watching television and getting as much exposure as possible.

Once you have the base memory, it will be very easy to memorize the words. By using this method, you can memorize the whole of the dictionary or crack any examination like GRE, GMAT or CAT; you can also become an excellent speaker articulating these words aptly.

Exercise

Below are a few words and their meanings. See if you can memorize them using the three-step process discussed above.

Bedizen	–	Dress up or decorate gaudily
Gambit	–	An act or remark that is calculated to gain an advantage, especially at the outset of a situation
Celestial	–	Positioned in or relating to the sky, or outer space as observed in astronomy
Diligent	–	Having or showing care and conscientiousness in one's work or duties
Rollick	–	Act or behave in a jovial and exuberant fashion
Cherub	–	A beautiful or innocent-looking child
Ripples	–	A small wave or series of waves on the surface of water
Dogmatize	–	Represent as an undeniable truth

EIGHT

NUMBER–SHAPE METHOD

The number–shape method is a very simple yet effective way of remembering lists of items in a specific order. For example, in a specific case, you need to remember the objects with respect to the number in a sequence and you have to recall them randomly—number-object or object-number. In such cases, you should use the number–shape method.

Read the names of objects below:

1. Football
2. Coke
3. Goddess
4. Rainbow
5. Kite
6. National flag
7. Fan
8. Computer
9. Chocolate
10. Pencil

The number–shape method helps you to create pictures in your mind, where the numbers represent images in the shape of numbers. These images form a compound image that also encodes what is to be remembered.

Here, to remember the numbers, you need to convert them

into pictures. The numbers represent some common shapes. Look at the shapes below, or you may create your own shapes for the numbers.

1. Pen, candle, stick
2. Duck, swan
3. Heart, bird
4. Boat
5. Hook
6. Whistle, Golf club
7. Lamp post, cliff edge
8. Hourglass
9. Lollypop, balloon with a string attached flying freely
10. Bat and ball

If you find that these images do not attract you or stick to your mind, you can change them for something more meaningful. Hence, the first step is to have a very strong and quick image for each number.

Now, you need to memorize these numbers and shapes. Later, connect these shapes with the objects given above—link pen and football, duck and Coke, bird and goddess, etc.

Here, you should follow the same method of association that you had done earlier. For example, playing football with a pen, the duck is drinking Coke, a goddess is flying a bird, rowing a boat, watching a rainbow, flying a kite with a hook, etc.

Now, associate these objects with the shapes. The next time you have to recall any object number wise, all you need to do is to recall the shape image for that number. Once you get the image, the connected object will come automatically to your mind. This way, you can recall the object randomly—top to bottom or bottom to top. The number represents the object, or the object represents the number—both become easy to recall.

 **Exercise**

Imagine you have to remember the names of some modern thinkers. Though full names are provided, your effort should be to remember their last names to the least.

Baruch Spinoza
John Locke
David Hume
George Berkeley
Immanuel Kant
Jean-Jacques Rousseau
G.W.F. Hegel
Søren Kierkegaard
Charles Robert Darwin
Karl Marx

Step 1

Since the names do not have pictures, first you need to convert them into images.

Spinoza	–	Sponge
Locke	–	Lock
Hume	–	Home
Berkeley	–	Bargain Lee
Kant	–	Kanth (Rajinikanth)
Rousseau	–	*Rassi* (rope in Hindi)
Hegel	–	Huge
Kierkegaard	–	Crack Guard
Darwin	–	Door-win
Marx	–	Marks

Step 2

Now, you need to associate the shapes of numbers with the corresponding persons' names. The reason you are associating the shapes with the images is that you will be able to recall them independently and in a sequence—top to bottom and bottom to top. Sometimes, from an exam point of view, we need to remember them in order. That is when this method will come handy.

1. Like pen is writing on a sponge.
2. A duck is opening a lock.
3. A bird is sleeping in its home.
4. Brett Lee is bargaining standing in a boat.
5. Rajinikanth is hanging by a hook.
6. A whistle is tied to a *rassi*.
7. Imagine a huge lamp post.
8. An hourglass is broken by crack guard.
9. A lollypop is given as a gift to the door that has won a competition.
10. For playing bat and ball, you should first get good marks in the school.

Try to visualize these images or you can come up with images of your own.

Another example:

We need to remember a list of these 10 countries in order.

USA, Russia, Germany, Saudi Arabia, Canada, France, Britain, Spain, India and Ukrain.

The first step is that we have to create an image for each country:

USA   –   Donald Trump

Russia	–	*Rassi*
Germany	–	Germs-many
Saudi Arabia	–	*Sau* Arabs
Canada	–	Kannada
France	–	Prawns
Britain	–	Britannia Biscuit
Spain	–	Pain
Indian	–	Narendra Modi
Ukrain	–	Ukku-rain

The second step is to associate these 10 images with the shape of each number in the same order.

If you are able to do it, you will be able to recall the names of all 10 countries in the same order and randomly. That is the advantage of the number–shape method.

NINE

NUMBER–VALUE METHOD

In the previous chapter, we discussed the number–shape method. We selected a shape for every number with which we associated an image that we needed to remember.

Similarly, some memory athletes follow the number–value method. They select a value for each number and fix that in their permanent memory. Then, with these permanent pictures, they associate the new words that they need to remember. For this method, select the image through either shape or value. For the rest, the process of memorizing remains the same.

Imagine, you have to remember the following objects in this sequence or randomly.

1. Kite
2. Pizza
3. Fish
4. Board
5. Laddu
6. Duster
7. Mobile
8. Pen
9. Bag
10. Swan

If the number-shape method seems difficult, you can use the

number–value method in the following manner:

1. King
2. Eyes
3. Monkeys
4. Car
5. Fingers
6. Cricket
7. Rainbow
8. Spider
9. Planets
10. Ravana or Dashavatara

You have to repeat the numbers and the values. Once this comes involuntarily to you, all you need to do is associate king and the kite, eyes and pizza, monkeys and fish, etc. This will take some practice. But once you perfect it, the numbers or the objects will become easy to recall in any order.

The number–shape method or the number–value method is also useful when you need to remember subsections of the constitution or legal sections.

It is also necessary to know that memory athletes across the globe follow various methods that they feel comfortable with. Hence you get to choose the method you will eventually follow.

TEN

NUMBER–RHYME METHOD

The number–rhyme method is a very simple way to remember a list of items in a specific order. Most of us have learnt the nursery rhyme, 'One, two, Buckle my shoe; Three, four, Knock at the door…' This nursery rhyme was so easy to memorize even as a child, because the numbers rhymed with the objects so well. The number–rhyme method follows the same formula.

This technique works by helping you to create pictures in your mind, in which the numbers are represented by things that rhyme with the number, and are linked to images that represent the things to be remembered.

Purpose

Obviously, your purpose is to remember a list of 10 unconnected or unrelated items, and to be able to recall them on demand in any order, at some time in the future. It is as useful as an instant notepad for a shopping list.

How It Works

For this, you will have to associate some of the new items—the item to be remembered—with something that you already know very well. For this to work, it is essential that you have the framework in place to which you can make the associations.

Imagine that you have to remember the following objects number wise.

1. Ring
2. Queen
3. Paper
4. Camera
5. Uniform
6. Sofa
7. Coffee
8. Crocodile
9. Watch
10. Chocolate

Framework

By using the following table, you can set up the permanent reference points that you will be using to make the associations.

The table lists the numbers 1 to 10, and a word that rhymes with each number, with a suggested image. Memorize the rhyming words and create a mental picture of each item. Do not proceed in the exercise until you are sure that you have done this.

Here you need permanent pictures for the numbers using a rhyming word. The new objects should be linked to the words formed with the help of the number–rhyme system.

Number	Rhyming Word		Rhyme-System Word/ Sound/Image
1	One	–	Run, Gun, Bun, Sun
2	Two	–	Zoo, Shoe
3	Three	–	Tree, Sea
4	Four	–	Door, Shore

5	Five	–	Hive, Drive
6	Six	–	Vicks, Sticks, Bricks
7	Seven	–	Heaven
8	Eight	–	Gate, Skate
9	Nine	–	Wine
10	Ten	–	Hen

You have to keep repeating these rhyming sounds with the corresponding numbers, until you are comfortable with them and they become easy to recall. Once the rhyming sounds become a part of your subconscious mind, you have to associate the given objects with the rhyming sound. For example, *run* and *ring*, *zoo* with *queen*, *tree* with *paper*, etc. Next time, if you need to recall the number of any object, you can do so by recalling the corresponding rhyming word. You will be able to remember the object and the number automatically.

Take a minute or so to visualize the item to be remembered with the rhyming word. If you make the picture appear funny or silly, it will create the best mental image. You could also use a cartoon and exaggerate one or more features of the object. Don't move on to the next item in the list until you have a clear image in your mind.

🧠 Exercise

Can you memorize the names of ten Greek philosophers in the right order?

1. Parmenides
2. Anaxagoras
3. Anaximander
4. Empedocles

5. Zeno
6. Pythagoras
7. Socrates
8. Plato
9. Heraclitus
10. Democritus

Step 1

The names have no images; so first, we should convert the names into some known images. Such as:

Parmenides	–	Permanently dies
Anaxagoras	–	Anna-grass
Anaximander	–	Alexander
Empedocles	–	Empty dose
Zeno	–	Zen
Pythagoras	–	Python
Socrates	–	Secret
Plato	–	Plate
Heraclitus	–	Hero
Democritus	–	Democrat

Step 2

Associate the rhymes with the names.

1. Burn a body and it permanently dies once.
2. Anna was walking on grass wearing shoes.
3. Alexander was climbing the trees.
4. Empty doses were lying on the door.
5. Zen car was going over the beehives.
6. Python was being hit with sticks.
7. You need to maintain secrets in heaven.
8. Plates are given at the gate.

9. Hero is drinking wine.
10. Democrats are catching hens.

You can try to visualize these scenarios as suggested or come up with ones of your own.

Once you have done this, try to write down the names of the philosophers on a piece of paper. You should be able to do this by thinking of the numbers denoted at the end of the sentence. Then, thinking about the part of the image associated with the number and then the whole image, and finally, decode the image to give you the name of the philosopher.

Applying the Number–Rhyme Method

You can use the system for creating the foundations for a specific subject area. For example, the above could be about ancient philosophy, as images representing the philosophers, systems and theories by each philosopher can now be associated with the images representing philosophers' names.

The sillier the image, the more effectively you will remember it.

ELEVEN

BODY PARTS METHOD

A location or a file is simply a place to store information. For example, the first building in your city files is your first file. All ten files work together in this filing system.

Anything can be a file system as long as it follows a logical order and you can visualize the item. For example, your car could be a file system with ten files. Number one is the front bumper, two is the engine, three is the front windshield, four is the steering wheel, five is the gearshift, six is the CD box, seven is the passenger seat, eight is the back seat, nine is the storage place and number ten is the number plate.

You are going to create a file system that I think you are going to like. There are ten files in this system, and they are referred to as your skeleton files. Why? Because the files are your body parts!

These are going to be permanent files for you, and you must call them what I call them. This may be the most important file system you have learned up to this point.

This system is a little different, but have fun with it:

- Number one? That is the top of your head.
- Number two? This is your nose, so pat your nose and say number two.
- Number three? This is your mouth. Say mouth and then touch your mouth.
- Number four? Your ribs.

- Number five? Your liver.
- Number six? This is your hip joint; you will call it joint.
- Number seven? This is your knee cap.
- Number eight? It is going to be a bone in our calves—the fibula. So, repeat after me. Number eight is fibula.
- Number nine is at the very bottom. It is the ball of your foot. You are going to call it ball.
- And number ten is not part of your skeleton; you will call it sand.

Now, you are going to go through the same process as you did with the city files. I am going to give you a list of words and you are going to memorize them using your body as the location to store the word. If you need to stop in between and ensure that you know your skeleton files, do that before proceeding.

Here is a list of ten items and files. Place the first one to your first skeleton file, the second one to your second skeleton file and so on. Move as fast as you can through this list. Force yourself to go faster than you think is possible and you will be amazed with your capability to recall. However, keep in mind that speed is not essential at this stage, understanding the system is.

- Speaker
- Gun
- Soldier
- Spotlight
- Amitabh Bachchan
- Judge
- Jury
- Money
- Fish
- Parliament

Review all ten quickly and attach them to your files as rapidly as you can. Do not take more than a minute to do this. So, how did you do? Did you get all ten? If not, ask yourself why. It could be one of two reasons—either you did not know your file, or your picture was not vivid enough.

Now, I think you will agree that these pictures were somewhat unusual. When you do this on your own, you have the freedom to make your own pictures. The skeleton file could be used to recall a things-to-do list, steps in a presentation, procedures, organization mission statements or to give a speech. The applications are endless. This system can truly change the way you go about your daily life if you let it.

Imagine, you have to recall the following objects with the corresponding numbers.

1. Jeep
2. Scale
3. Water
4. Bed
5. Eraser
6. Cycle
7. Dictionary
8. Revolver
9. Dosa
10. Pen
11. Bat
12. Newspaper
13. Key
14. Lotus
15. Dustbin

We are very comfortable with our body and its parts. When you have more than 10 items, you may use the following body parts as well. We have to imagine all parts of our body in the sequential order as shown below:

1. Hair
2. Head
3. Forehead
4. Eyebrow
5. Eyes
6. Ears
7. Nose
8. Mouth
9. Cheeks
10. Chin
11. Neck
12. Chest
13. Hands
14. Stomach
15. Legs

Once, you are familiar with these, you need to associate the objects and the body parts sequentially. Associate *jeep* and *hair*, *scale* and *head*, *water* and *forehead,* etc. The next time you should be able to recall the object and number or the number and object by simply recalling the association.

TWELVE

HOUSE METHOD

In this chapter, we will create some new files. I use this filing system most of the time. It is called house files. This is similar to city files, only in this case, we use rooms or areas of our house as 'files' to store information/memory.

In this method, you need to select five rooms or sections in your house. (If you live in a small apartment, you can have five sections—a bathroom, a kitchen, a living room, a hall and a bedroom.) Now, visualize yourself standing near the main door of your first room. Then start choosing five files from each room from the right or left, it does not matter, just so you are consistent. You could go clockwise or anti-clockwise too. Say your first room is the bedroom; you could select five pieces of furniture in there. The next room could be the kitchen in which you pick five appliances. The next could be the bathroom, and so on. Pick big items over small items and spread them across the room evenly and avoid using the same items for each room.

I have created these mental journeys in every home I have ever lived in. I have also created journeys through my friends' homes. You should do the same as this will be a great exercise for you too. You could easily create 200–300 files in just a few hours.

Now, for the instruction on how to do this: The first room should have one to five, the second room should have six to ten, the third room should have eleven to fifteen, the fourth room should have sixteen to twenty, and the fifth room should have twenty to twenty-five. The best thing that you could do right now is create and review these twenty-five files until you know them without making any mistakes—both the number and the file.

How to Use This Method

This also follows the same steps as the others. Once we have fixed 25 key locations, attach one word or one object to be memorized with each file. You can easily recall all the 25 points in the same order.

Now, you will learn a bit about product knowledge. You will use your house files for this purpose. You have five rooms and five files in each room. You will become an automobile salesperson today. However, this would work effectively even if you did not sell cars. As a salesperson, you not only want to know the features of your product, but you also want to know the benefits of similar models competitors may have.

You dedicate your first room to the product knowledge (which could be anything). Pick five key selling features of your product and file them. Your focus will be on sports utility vehicles and you are a Toyota salesperson. Take the five selling features and file them in your first room. For example, legroom to one file, financing to another and sunroof to another. Whatever the five key selling features are, file them in your first five files.

But, what are the other four rooms for? Each one of these rooms is dedicated to your competition. In each one of these rooms, list the five benefits of your car over theirs.

If you so desire, you could fill up all twenty-five files with information on your product. The reason I threw in competition information is that people are comfortable doing business with the salesperson who knows about the sales industry, including how their product measures up to the competition.

I recall studying for a psychology test one day, and in the first room, I filed five major psychologists. I used the second room to file theories. The third room was for experiments, and I continued until I had all my notes arranged into files.

Similarly, you could customize your notes of files. For example, if you are a student or a business professional, the room files are a great way to group thoughts or ideas by room. It helps to organize them in your mind.

If you need to recall the information about a product, use your house files if you are a salesperson who needs to file information about a product. It may take a moment to sit down and do it. However, even if you are a veteran sales professional, I think you will be astounded at the amount of new information you can store.

If you are in the field of business, filing information will be integral to your job. It could be procedures or new kinds of training. If you are a student, you should get out your notes for the next test and file them in your twenty-five house files. Remember that you can group them by rooms. Fill up your twenty-five files with something that is going to be a benefit to you.

World Memory Competition

In the National and World Memory Competitions, we call this method as location or loci method or memory palace method as well. We need to fix some pieces of furniture or locations first. Use this method to assign the spoken numbers, images or playing cards. We have an image for each card and that image is associated with that particular piece of furniture or location.

When we take the same journey again, we are able to recall each image. This works very beautifully. All top memory athletes have locations amounting to 1000 and above to store data.

THIRTEEN

ALPHABET METHOD

We learnt the 26 letters of the English Alphabet—from A to Z—as children.

To reinforce the same, our teachers gave us a word for each letter. For example, A for Apple, B for Bat and C for Cat, etc. Hence, all the English letters became very easy for us to reproduce.

Now, we are going to use this alphabet method in memory to remember objects in sequence.

I had used this method to memorize 200 random words in my First Guinness World Record.

We learn different methods in order to keep things interesting and not monotonous; also, fresh associations are easy to recall.

The alphabet method is a basic method used for remembering long lists of items in a specific order in such a way so that the missing items can be detected.

Imagine that you have to recall the following objects number wise, from top to bottom, bottom to top, or in a random order.

1. Tree
2. Railway station
3. Fish
4. Bucket
5. Scooter
6. Battery
7. Potato

8. Computer
9. Electric pole
10. Tiger
11. Suitcase
12. Television
13. Michael Jackson
14. Wooden sofa
15. Rabbit
16. ID Card
17. Paper
18. Road
19. Building
20. Mother
21. Nelson Mandela
22. Cricket match
23. Chennai
24. Refrigerator
25. Shirt
26. Globe

How to Use the Alphabet Method

The alphabet method is the simple method you had learnt during your early schooldays. This is how your teachers taught you to remember letters.

For this technique, you need to associate the images represented and cued by the letters of the alphabet, with the images that represent items to be remembered.

The selection of images representing letters may be based on the first letters, phone or in such a way that the sound of the first syllable of the image word is the name of the letter. E.g., you could represent the letter 'k' with the word 'kite'.

It is best to select the strongest images that come to mind

and stick with them. See below:

Number	Alphabet	Alphabet Words
1	A	Aeroplane
2	B	Balloon
3	C	Car
4	D	Dog
5	E	Elephant
6	F	Fire
7	G	Goat
8	H	Head
9	I	Inkpot
10	J	Jackfruit
11	K	Knife
12	L	Laddoo
13	M	Monkey
14	N	Newspaper
15	O	Oil
16	P	Postbox
17	Q	Queen
18	R	Railway Station
19	S	Shoes
20	T	Telephone
21	U	Umbrella
22	V	Velvet
23	W	Water
24	X	Xmas tree
25	Y	Yellow chalk piece
26	Z	Zoo

I am sure you know these words your teachers or parents taught you. You have to be perfect with the letter and the word. Later, you need to relate to the alphabet and the number. Like letter 'O' stands for 'oil', which is number 15. Letter 'U' stands for 'umbrella', which is number 21.

If you find that these images do not stick in your mind, you may change them for something else that is more meaningful to you.

Once you visualize them firmly and link them to their root letters, these images can be linked to the things to be remembered.

Now you need to associate object number 1, tree, with aeroplane; object number 2, railway station, with balloon and so on. The method of association will remain the same. All you are doing is trying to have different sets of permanent pictures for each number. Next time, it will be easy for you to tell the number of the object or if you are asked a number, you will be able to tell the object.

The alphabet system is the most difficult and complex method of memorizing. However, it is more powerful as it allows you to code and remember a list of up to 26 items.

I personally use this method for memory demonstrations during my training sessions. It works beautifully for me. You may try it too and explore how beautifully it works.

FOURTEEN

SYMBOLIZATION METHOD

This method of codification is used to transform abstract nouns into visual images. An abstract noun can have several visual representations in your mind. Choose the image that suits you best.

Try to remember the following words:

1. Cold
2. Warm
3. Illness
4. Eternity
5. Separation
6. Infinity
7. Autumn
8. Winter
9. Summer

There are no images for such abstract words. In such cases, you have to choose an appropriate word/image/symbol. You must choose an image that comes easily to you, one that appears first in your brain. If you find it difficult to choose an image to suit a word, it means you do not understand the word.

For example, look at the words below:

Cold	–	Ice
Warm	–	hot water

Illness	–	Thermometer
Eternity	–	Egyptian pyramids
Separation	–	Train
Infinity	–	unending long line
Autumn	–	Leaves
Winter	–	Snow
Summer	–	Skates

Associate the symbols with abstract words and memorize the chosen images. When you recollect the images to test yourself, write the original word down.

Try to memorize the following abstract words:

Exercise 1

	Attempt No. 1	**Attempt No. 2**
Pain		
Richness		
Sadness		
Poverty		
Separation		
Space		
Time		
Philosophy		
Love		
Friendship		
Fun		
Eternity		
Cold		
Spring		

Jealousy		
Trouble		
Luck		

Exercise II

	Attempt No. 1	Attempt No. 2
Accuracy		
Nonsense		
Rage		
Attention		
Pride		
Speed		
Tenderness		
Politeness		
Heat		
Humidity		
Run		
Look		
Admire		
Enjoy		
Trust		
Reflection		
Hatred		
Diligence		
Carelessness		
Calm		

You must convert the above-mentioned abstract words in to meanings (images) that come to you instantly. Memorize them using the visualization method. When you recall these words, you must pause for a second and get the actual word instead of the one you memorized.

Subject Names

You should choose the images that come instantly to you when you think about these subjects. See examples below.

Mathematics	–	Graph
History	–	Napoleon
Drawing	–	Paint
Music	–	Flute
Geometry	–	Compass
English	–	William Shakespeare
Literature	–	Book
Gym Class	–	Weights

FIFTEEN

CONSONANCE METHOD

Any word that does not evoke visual images in your mind can be coded by consonance, i.e., by other words. They sound (but bringing visual images) similar to the words to be remembered, and thus, are more convenient to memorize.

Factor	–	Tractor
Kub	–	Cuba
Ricca	–	Rekha
Fian	–	Fan

Transform the words into visual images using the method of codifying by consonance. Memorize the perceived images using the visualization method. When you recall the images, write the original words down. You do not have to memorize their meanings, you only have to reproduce the words with their correct spellings.

Can you convert these words into some images?

1. Slate
2. Dool
3. Marc
4. Sat
5. Kano

6. Peir
7. Arsc
8. Pind
9. Roys
10. Bys
11. Zoor
12. Ded

When you memorize using this method, you need to focus on the goal of memorization. This is about not only recalling some words, but also their correct spellings. Thus, when you use 'Rekha' to memorize 'Ricca', you have to make sure that you get the right spelling. This normally happens when people have some knowledge of what they are studying and they would easily be able to recall the right spelling.

In the National and World Memory Championships, memorizing words is one of the 10 memory disciplines. Twenty words are given in a column. Some of these are proper nouns and some are abstract words. We use this method to convert the words into images we can visualize. We get the correct word when the image appears. All memory athletes need to practise a lot to perfect this method, as the rules of corrections are very strict. For example, you get 20 marks for getting all 20 words right in a column. If you get one word wrong, the score comes down to 10. If you get two or more words wrong in a column, your score will be zero. Hence, one has to be very careful in memorizing the right word with the right spelling as well.

Memorizing Letters

Many times, letters A to Z form a part of a vehicle's registration number or legal subsections, the Indian Penal Code or the Articles of the constitution. For such things, you should simply associate the letters with pictures that you learnt as children. This has been discussed earlier in depth in the alphabet method. The codes will be as follows:

A	–	Aeroplane
B	–	Balloon
C	–	Car
D	–	Dog
E	–	Elephant
F	–	Fire
G	–	Goat
H	–	Head or a heater
I	–	Inkpot
J	–	Jackfruit
K	–	Knife
L	–	Laddu
M	–	Monkey
N	–	Newspaper
O	–	Oil
P	–	Postbox
Q	–	Queen
R	–	Railway station
S	–	Shoe
T	–	Telephone
U	–	Umbrella
V	–	Velvet
W	–	Water
X	–	Xmas tree
Y	–	Yellow chalk piece
Z	–	Zoo or Zebra

SIXTEEN

MNEMONIC METHOD

By now, you must have noticed that whenever the technique—Association, Linking or Imagination—is used, you have different items from different categories. These can be anything—a person's name, a vegetable, a fruit, a country, an animal, a bird, an action or a character. In such cases, it becomes easy for us to make an association. Imagine that we only had items belonging to a single category—all persons, all countries, all vegetables, all fruits, all birds, all animals or all characters. It would have become difficult to make up a story then. This is where the story or visualization method ends, and the mnemonic method begins.

This method is used when a number of items belong to the same group/category and for science subjects where visualization becomes difficult. For example:

(a) Seven Colours of a Rainbow: Violet, Indigo, Blue, Green, Yellow, Orange, Red

You remember them by VIBGYOR. What you have done here is, you have taken the first letter from each colour and tried to make a meaningful word. The moment you remember VIBGYOR, you know with V comes Violet, with I comes Indigo, with B comes Blue, with G comes Green, with Y comes Yellow, with O comes Orange and with R comes Red.

You will be able to recall all the colours of the rainbow very easily.

But, the question is how to remember 'VIBGYOR'? What if you forget the word itself!

The answer is very simple. Imagine you are to travel to some other city; carrying all the clothes, toiletries and other items separately will be so difficult. Even if you manage to carry all of them, you might run out of space to store them, and as you get off the train, you might misplace something or forget something. However, if you keep them all in a single bag, it will be very easy to carry so many items, to store the bag in the train and it will be easier remember to carry just one bag.

Now, you might ask what if I forget that one bag and get off the train.

When you pack items yourself and keep in the bag, you will remember to carry it with you.

Similarly, when you think and make your own mnemonic devices, they remain in your memory for a long time.

Let us try to find a better solution than the one we already have. In this competitive world, the person who learns to reach the goal faster is the winner.

Imagine that people could only walk. But if you learnt to ride a bicycle, you would have reached your destination sooner than those who could only walk.

Again, if you were to learn to ride a bike, you would reach your destination faster than the rest.

Therefore, it is all about learning, fine-tuning and mastering the memory techniques that will help you receive, store and retrieve information faster than the others.

Let us see a few more examples of the mnemonic method:

Planets of the Solar System:

Mercury, Venus, Earth, Mars, Jupiter, Saturn, Uranus and Neptune

I remember these names with the help of this sentence: 'My Very Enthusiastic Mother Just Served Us Noodles.'

Also, you must have read these basic mnemonic devices in your school. Let us see if you can recall them:

In Mathematics, BODMAS stands for...............
In Trigonometry, All Silver Tea Cups stands for..............

Develop mnemonics for the following:

1. Union Territories of India (Chandigarh, Delhi, Puducherry, Daman & Diu, Lakshadweep, Andaman and Nicobar Islands and Dadra and Nager Haveli)
   CLAP D3
2. Parts of speech (Pronoun, Adjective, Verb, Adverb, Noun, Preposition, Interjection and Conjunction)
   PAVAN PIC
3. 12 zodiac signs (Aries, Taurus, Gemini, Cancer, Leo, Virgo, Libra, Scorpion, Sagittarius, Capricorn, Aquarius and Pisces)
   CLASS VGP TALC
4. Names of countries larger than India (China, Australia, Russia, Canada, USA and Brazil)
   CAR CUB
5. Seven continents (Europe, Antarctica, Asia, Africa, Australia, North America and South America)
   Eat An Apple After A Nice Sleep
6. Reactivity series (Potassium, Sodium, Calcium, Magnesium, Aluminium, Carbon, Zinc, Iron, Lead, Hydrogen, Copper, Silver and Gold)
   Please Stop Calling Me A Cute Zebra I Like Her Calling Me Smart Goat. Pranam–Thanks
7. Cranial nerves (Olfactory, Optic, Occulomotor,

Pathetic, Trigeminal, Abducens, Facial, Auditory, Glassopharyngeal, Vagus, Spinal Accessory and Hypoglossal)

On Occasion of Party, the Attractive Faces are Girl Visitors Says Harry, or Oh! Oh! Oh! Please Touch and Find All Grains Very Small Hands.

8. 10 organ systems (nervous system, integumentary system, circulatory system, endocrinal system, respiratory system, digestive system, reproductive system, immune system, muscular system, skeletal system and urinary system)
   NIICER DRUMS

9. Colour codes of a resistor (Black, Brown, Red, Orange, Yellow, Grey, Blue, Violet, Grey and White)
   BBROY Great Britain Very Good Wife

Use this method in your textbooks to remember any list. Prepare your own mnemonic devices.

SEVENTEEN

MEMORIZING NUMBERS I

This is going to be a skill, which if mastered, will astound people. I am going to show you how to memorize a 100-digit number after just hearing it once.

When I do my memory demonstrations, I take a 100-digit number and memorize it forwards, backwards and row and column wise. I use this skill to memorize phone numbers, bank account numbers, etc.

This is somewhat at an advanced level. So do not worry if it does not make sense the first time. It is something that you may have to review three or four times to understand.

People find it difficult to memorize numbers, as numbers do not have pictures. Numbers are abstract and must be turned into pictures before you can recall them.

This system was actually introduced more than 300 years ago by Stonsen Mink Vonwesenhein. Dr Richard Gray, an Englishman, modified Vonwesenhein's basic construction. The phonetic system was devised to allow the master memorizers of the time to break the bonds of the previously excellent, but more limited systems. This system was developed to memorize long digit numbers.

Basically, there are only 10 digits—1,2,3,4,5,6,7,8,9,0.

For every number from one to nine and zero (total ten), a consonant sound is assigned. The sounds have been assigned to them over hundreds of years since the time of Dr Richard Gray. Here they are:

Number		Sound
1	–	T or D
2	–	N
3	–	M
4	–	R
5	–	L
6	–	J, Ch, Sh
7	–	K, C, G
8	–	F, V
9	–	P, B
10	–	Z, S

For some numbers, more than one sound is assigned. There is no logic behind this, but it is only a matter of convenience. Hence only a single number and a single sound are given for you to use. But, when more than one sound is provided, you may use any one of these sounds; whichever you find is easy to remember and could recall quickly.

All you have to do is memorize these. Does that sound like a challenge? What if I told you that these could be learnt in less than a minute? What if I told you that you have already memorized them? That is right! You have already memorized these. I already taught you these numbers.

Remember when I told you that everything in this book is said for a reason and I am actually going to teach you things that you are not even using yet? Well, here is an example of that. Do you remember what you learnt in the body part method? Let us review the files.

Top, nose, mouth, ribs, liver, joint, cap, fibula, ball and sand.

Now, let us review the phonetic sounds. They are: T, N, M, R, L, J, K, F, P and S. Did you catch that? Let us go slow this time.

- The sound assigned to number one is T or D, and the first skeleton file is *top*.
- The letter assigned to number two is N because it has the N sound and the second skeleton file is *nose*. So two is N.
- The letter assigned to the number three is M and our third skeleton file is *mouth*. Three is M.
- The letter assigned to four is R. The fourth skeleton file is *ribs*. Four is R.
- The fifth skeleton file is *liver*, and the letter assigned to number five is L. Five is L.
- Six is J, CH or SH and the sixth skeleton file is *joint*. *Joint* represents the J.
- The seventh file is a hard C sound, or K or G. And the seventh skeleton file is *cap*. Seven is a hard C or a K.
- The letter assigned to the number eight is F or V. Your eighth skeleton file is your *fibula*. Number eight is F or V.
- The letter assigned to number nine is P or B. And your ninth skeleton file is *ball*. So, number nine is P or B.
- And finally, the last skeleton file is actually number ten, but for the purposes of this system, this will represent the number zero. Zero is assigned to S or Z. Zero is the Z sound. So here, S stands for *Sand*.

Now stop and review your skeleton files and make sure that you know the sounds—one through 10 where 10 actually represents zero. Make sure that you know them.

 **Exercise**

1. Convert the following numbers into sounds:

2	4	6	7	8	5	7	9	0	1
3	1	0	8	0	9	8	0	3	2
4	5	4	8	2	2	0	1	3	6
1	5	4	6	2	1	5	5	7	4
1	2	5	4	7	8	9	1	2	3

2. Convert the following sounds into numbers:

P	S	D	F	G	V	B	N	K	P
L	O	I	J	M	N	H	G	B	Y
S	L	I	J	N	B	G	T	R	F
U	T	R	E	W	Q	A	S	D	R
H	G	H	Y	F	H	J	M	I	Y

Memorizing Numbers I • 97

3. Convert these words into numbers:

S.No.	Words	Numbers
1	Printer	
2	Computer	
3	Rocket	
4	Confidence	
5	Freedom	
6	Arrest	
7	Cover	
8	People	
9	Practice	
10	Institute	
11	Sania Mirza	
12	DhoniNayak	
13	Village	
14	Minister	
15	Parent	
16	Microsoft	
17	Yellow	
18	Red colour	
19	Knowledge	
20	Physics	
21	Love	
22	Doormat	
23	Water bottle	
24	Exam pad	
25	School bus	

4. Convert the following numbers into pictures using the phonetic method:

9	
0	
10	
4	
30	
78	
47	
100	
66	
24	
35	
08	

So, how did you do? Is this taking you some time to get used to? If it seems a little unusual to you, do not worry about it! However, most likely you have never attempted to memorize a 100-digit number. Below are some of the permanent pictures for the numbers that you can use:

1	–	Day
2	–	Knee
3	–	*Maa*
4	–	Rai
5	–	Law
6	–	Jaw
7	–	Key
8	–	Fee
9	–	Bee

10	–	Dosa
11	–	Daddy
12	–	Don
13	–	Dam
14	–	Door
15	–	Doll
16	–	Dish
17	–	Dog
18	–	Deaf
19	–	Deep
20	–	Nose
21	–	Net
22	–	Nun
23	–	Neem
24	–	Nehru
25	–	Nail
26	–	*Naach*
27	–	Neck
28	–	Knife
29	–	Nib
30	–	Mass
31	–	Mat
32	–	Moon
33	–	Mummy
34	–	*Mor*
35	–	Mall
36	–	Mesh
37	–	Mike
38	–	Movie
39	–	Map
40	–	Rose
41	–	Road

42	–	Run
43	–	Rum
44	–	Roar
45	–	Rail
46	–	Raja
47	–	Rock
48	–	Roof
49	–	Rope
50	–	Lassi
51	–	Laddu
52	–	Lion
53	–	Lime
54	–	Lorry
55	–	Laila
56	–	Leach
57	–	Lake
58	–	Leaf
59	–	Lab
60	–	Chess
61	–	*Jaadu*
62	–	John
63	–	Jam
64	–	Jar
65	–	Jail
66	–	Chacha
67	–	Jockey
68	–	Java
69	–	Jeep
70	–	Kiss
71	–	Kite
72	–	Cane
73	–	Cam

Memorizing Numbers I • 101

74	–	Car
75	–	Coal
76	–	Cash
77	–	Cake
78	–	Coffee
79	–	Cap
80	–	Fuse
81	–	Fat
82	–	Fan
83	–	FM
84	–	Fire
85	–	Fool
86	–	Fish
87	–	Fog
88	–	FIFA
89	–	VIP
90	–	Bus
91	–	Bat
92	–	Bun
93	–	PM
94	–	Bar
95	–	Ball
96	–	Bush
97	–	Bike
98	–	Puff
99	–	Baba
100	–	Disease
0	–	Zoo
00	–	Sauce
01	–	Soda
02	–	Sun
03	–	SIM card

102 • *The Ultimate Guide to Master Your Memory*

04	–	Saree
05	–	Sail
06	–	*Soch*
07	–	Sack
08	–	Sofa
09	–	Soap

These numbers above and the images are also called permanent images or peg words. We have to repeat them so often that the moment we say a number, the image flashes in front of our eyes. This is the basic exercise one has to do to memorize numbers. The process will take some time, but it is going to be worth the time and effort.

 Exercise 1

What if you had to remember a 40-digit number when you finished converting the numbers into pictures?

2 4 4 9 3 2 7 8 0 4 6 9 2 8 6 2 1 0 8 4 9 4 1 1 1 8 5 5 9 6 7 0 7 2 6 5 0 9 9 2

It is difficult to remember such a number. We have to break them into groups of two digits. Convert the 2-digit numbers into pictures. Make up a story and you will have all the numbers forwards and backwards as well.

For example, let us convert the numbers given above into pictures:

24 – Nehru, 49 – Rope, 32 – Moon, 78 – Kaif, 04 – Saree,
69 – Jeep, 28 – Knife, 62 – John, 10 – Dosa, 84 – Fire,
94 – Bar, 11 – Daddy, 18 – TV, 55 – Laila, 96 – Bush,
70 – Kiss, 72 – Gun, 65 – Jail, 09 – Soap, 92 – Bun

Use visualization method to remember the words: Imagine *Nehru* was holding a *rope* and he reached the *Moon*. He saw *Kaif* in a *saree*. He got into a *jeep* and drove off. Holding a *knife* in his hand, *John* stopped and attacked him. Nehru made a *dosa* and John set *fire* on him. Then John went to a *bar* for a drink. Your *Daddy* was watching *TV* there. John Saw *Laila* and *Bush kissing*. John took out his *gun* and fired at them. He was taken to *jail*. There he took a bath with a *soap*, then ate a *bun* and slept.

You will be able to recall all the numbers with this story. Try for yourself.

EIGHTEEN

MASTERING NUMBERS II

Let us go a little deeper into phonetics. The best way to practise phonetics is that every time you hear a number, you must turn the number into a picture instantly. When you drive to work today and happen to see Exit 53, turn it into a picture. Say to yourself, five is L and three is M; it is a lime!

Initially, you are going to have to go through the steps when you want to turn 53 into a picture. However, it comes to you automatically the next time. When you hear numbers later, you will no longer be turning them into a picture. You already have the pictures available.

Here are 35 pictures and you are going to add them to your files. Each of these pictures represents a number. Set a timer for five minutes for this next exercise. You will memorize 35 pictures (70 digits, as each picture will have two digits) in five minutes. Do not beat yourself up if you do not get them all, but let us aim for it.

1. Nail
2. Can
3. Chess
4. Moon
5. Mail
6. Match
7. Bus
8. Tin

9. Fire
10. Chef
11. Mop
12. Pool
13. Ship
14. Dove
15. Cat
16. Pipe
17. Dish
18. Shin
19. Tyre
20. Dish
21. Jet
22. Rat
23. Mom
24. Foam
25. Kiss
26. Rat
27. Pan
28. Pack
29. Nap
30. Leash
31. Mall
32. Jar
33. File
34. Leaf
35. Shack

Now, stop and write these words (1–35) down. You just memorized 35 pictures (70-digit number). Here it is:

1.	Nail	–	25
2.	Can	–	72
3.	Chess	–	60

4.	Moon	–	32
5.	Mail	–	35
6.	Match	–	36
7.	Bus	–	90
8.	Tin	–	12
9.	Fire	–	84
10.	Chef	–	68
11.	Mop	–	39
12.	Pool	–	95
13.	Ship	–	69
14.	Dove	–	18
15.	Cat	–	71
16.	Pipe	–	99
17.	Dish	–	16
18.	Shin	–	62
19.	Tyre	–	14
20.	Fish	–	86
21.	Jet	–	61
22.	Rat	–	41
23.	Mom	–	33
24.	Foam	–	83
25.	Kiss	–	70
26.	Rat	–	41
27.	Pan	–	92
28.	Pack	–	97
29.	Nap	–	29
30.	Leash	–	56
31.	Mail	–	35
32.	Jar	–	64
33.	File	–	85
34.	Leaf	–	58
35.	Shack	–	67

How did you do? Perfect score? Did you get close? This is fun, isn't it?

Convert the following mobile number into a picture:
Jayasimha: 9866018989

98	–	puff
66	–	*Chacha*
01	–	soda
89	–	VIP
89	–	VIP

Now, make up a short story related to me: Jayasimha eats a vegetable *puff* every day. His *Chacha* came to give him a *soda*. Everyone says that he is a VIP. If you can associate this with me, you will be able to recall my number very easily.

Exercise

(a) Write down your family members' mobile numbers and remember them by using the same method:

_____

_____

(b) Remember the following vehicle numbers and Bank ATM pin numbers using the same method:

9136 ———, 2462 ———, 5432 ———,
7195 ———, 9733 ———, 603 ———,
555 ———, 254 ———, 4511 ———,
8526 ———, 568 ———, 6819 ———,

(c) Now, remember your bike/car number and bank ATM pin numbers.

_____

_____

(d) Remembering historical years:

- 1914–1918—First World War
  Here, you can safely eliminate the century, as you are very much aware of it. You have to convert 14 and 18 into pictures and associate with the First World War.
  14—door, 18—deaf
  Now imagine, during the First World War, people were fighting with wooden doors. They kept hitting each other until they went deaf and the War stopped.

- 1939–1945—Second World War
  Leaving the century, let us convert 39 and 45 into pictures.
  39—MP, 45—Rail
  Imagine, during the Second World War, all the MPs came to fight. In the end, they came to an agreement and went back to their countries by rail and the War stopped.

- 1968—H.G. Khorana was awarded the Nobel Prize
  68—Jail,
  Khorana—*Quran*, the holy book of Islam. (Convert the name into an image)
  Just imagine, in jail, he taught the *Quran* to everybody. Hence, he was awarded Nobel Prize.

- 1927—Simon Commission
  27—Knife
  Imagine, when the Simon Commission was implemented, people started protesting with big knives.

- 1942—Quit India Movement.
  Here, convert 42 into a picture—Run
  Imagine, Mahatma Gandhi started the Quit India Movement and all ran away.

Let us take one chapter from history on Napoleon.

Year	Occurrence
1769	Birth
1792	French Revolution
1795	National Convention Revolt
1798	Egypt Campaign
1799	Consulate Government
1804	Emperor
1813	Battle of Nations
1814	Elba
1815	Waterloo
1821	Demise

Imagine, when Napoleon was *born*, he was driving a *jeep* (1769). The *French Revolution* happened for the need of a *bun* (1792). The *National Meeting* was convened to reduce *belly* (1795). Napoleon went to *Egypt* to eat a *puff* (1798). He consolidated his position by dressing up like a *Baba* (1799). When he became an *Empower*, he was wearing a *saree* (1804). When all the countries came to attack France, a '*dom, dom*' (1813) sound was heard from the battlefields. His *elbow* (Elba) hit the *door* (1814). He drank water and went to the *Loo* (Waterloo) because he felt *dull* (1815). Finally, he died inside the *net* (1821).

This way, we can memorize one chapter of history within a short span of time.

Now, write a list of all the historical years from your textbook. Convert them into pictures and try to remember them:

_____
_____
_____

(e) Constants:
Melting point of Lead is 327.

- 327 (MNK)—A monkey is eating lead and melting.
- Silver melts at 1950.
  1950 (TBLS)(Tables)—Dad is making tables with silver.
- Height of Mt Everest is 8848 m
  8848 (FFRF)(FIFA-Roof)—Imagine everyone is climbing the Mt Everest carrying a football to play on a roof.
- Northernmost latitude
  37.6 (MKS)—Moksh
- Southernmost Latitude
  8.4 (FR)—Fire
- Easternmost Longitude
  97.25 (BKNL)—Bike and Nail
- Westernmost Longitude
  68.7 (Ch F G)—Chef-Go
- Atomic Mass Unit of Mercury
  201 (NST)—Nest

Now, write down all the constants/melting points/values from your textbook. Convert them into pictures and try to remember them.

_____
_____

NINETEEN

MEMORIZING BINARY NUMBERS

In the previous chapter, we discussed how to memorize normal numbers. Therefore, you had a phonetic sound for all the digits using which you were able to convert them into pictures and were able to make up a story. Didn't it seem a little simpler after a bit of practice?

Now, let us talk about how to memorize binary numbers.

Imagine you were given a list of binary numbers: 01010101 0111000101010110101010001100110101000101010101010000000.

You need to memorize the digits in order. But the problem is that the binary numbers constitute two digits—0 and 1—which reoccur.

If you try to form pictures on the basis of the previous exercise with normal numbers, the pictures formed will be as follows:

01–soda
01–soda
01–soda
01–soda
01–soda
11–dada
10–dosa
00–sauce
10–dosa
10–dosa
11–dada

And so on so forth.

To create a story with the same repeated images will be very difficult. Hence, you cannot use this method for memorizing binary numbers. The only way to memorize them is to convert them into normal numbers. To do so, you need to take three binary digits at once instead of two.

A pattern will begin to emerge when you take three digits.

If you look at the pattern, you will realize that basically there are 8 patterns:

000
001
010
011
100
101
110
111

You need to assign one normal number to each digit.

000—0, 001—1, 010—2, 011—3, 100—4, 101—5, 110—6, 111—7

The means by which these numbers are derived is very simple.

Unit's place value is 1, ten's place value is 2, hundred's place value is 4.

For example, if you have to find the value of 000, then, $0\times4+0\times2+0\times1 = 0$

001 will become $0\times4+0\times2+1\times1 = 1$
010 will become $0\times4+1\times2+0\times1 = 2$
011 will become $0\times4+1\times2+1\times1 = 3$
100 will become $1\times4+0\times2+0\times1 = 4$
101 will become $1\times4+0\times2+1\times1 = 5$
110 will become $1\times4+1\times2+0\times1 = 6$

111 will become 1×4+1×2+1×1 = 7

You will only get combinations.

Now, let us take the number given above: 0101010101110001 01010110101010001100110101000101010101010000000. Here, you need to convert groups of three digits into one normal digit. See below:

010—2, 101—5, 010—2, 111—7, 000—0, 101—5, 010—2, 110—6, 101—5, 010—2, 001—1, 100—4, 110—6, 101—5, 000—0, 101—5, 010—2, 101—5, 000— 0, 000—0.

Let us write the numbers down: 25270526521465052500

So, now you have converted them into normal numbers.

Next, use the phonetic method and convert these normal numbers into pictures. Take numbers together and convert each combination into an image.

25	–	Nail
27	–	Neck
05	–	Sail
26	–	*Naach*
52	–	Lion
14	–	Door
65	–	Jail
05	–	Sail
25	–	Nail
00	–	Sauce

Then, use the imagination method, or loci method or personalized memory system method (to be discussed) to remember these numbers.

To recall them, reconvert the pictures into normal numbers, and from there to binary numbers.

This process seems to be little difficult. However, once you start practising, this becomes very easy. As you know, I have set two Guinness World Records in memorizing binary numbers and you too can do it with just a little practice.

This method can be used in computer programming, and most importantly, the brain becomes so creative that your concentration, retention and ability to recall go up and this finally leads to a phenomenal memory.

TWENTY

PERSONALIZED MEMORY SYSTEM

Now, let us discuss a simple method of memorizing the objects that I had developed. This method is the most profound and powerful of all methods. All my Guinness World Records in Memory were won using this method.

When it comes to memory, our brain does not remember what we see, read, write, listen, do or experience. If I ask you, what you had for breakfast on 5 January 2017, you may not be able to recall. Many times, when you travel by an auto, train or bus, you do not remember the faces of all the auto drivers, TTEs or bus conductors.

However, imagine that you had breakfast with the prime minister or your favourite actor on 5 January, you will definitely remember this for a long time. Imagine, that you lost your bag in an auto or a train on 10 August 2016, and the auto driver or the TTE returned it to you. You will remember the face of this person. The reason is that emotions are involved here.

Emotions play a very important role in memory.

Mahatma Gandhi led the Dandi March. You read and forgot about it because there is no personal emotion involved in the incident. King Ashok fought the Kalinga war. You read this too, but also forgot about it due to the lack of personal connect with the war.

Imagine that you had led the Dandi March. You would have

certainly remembered this. If you had fought the Kalinga war yourself, you would have remembered the war vividly.

Hence, you need to involve yourself or have people who are related to you, such as your family members, school friends, office colleagues, neighbours or role models, to create these emotions. This method works on the aspect of creating emotions so that the impressions thus created in the brain are stronger.

These emotions are not created by objects but by people. You have a list of 100 people. This may include your family, relatives, friends, colleagues or acquaintances. All these people are numbered serially in some order so that we are able to recall the person and the number.

It will take some time to master this method, but once you master it, remembering text, numbers, speeches or any kind of data will become really easy.

For example, imagine you have to remember the following objects in a random order:

1. Telephone
2. Pepsi
3. Popcorn
4. Train
5. Pen
6. Hero Honda
7. Bible
8. Black board
9. London
10. Florist
11. Bread
12. Zoo
13. Laptop
14. Diamond

15. Trivandrum Beach
16. Mike
17. Car
18. Astrologer
19. Vivekananda
20. School Bag

In the personalized memory power system, you have to create 100 names of people, to whom you are close or are familiar with. So follow the categories and conditions below to create a personalized memory system of your own.

Categories in this system are:

- Names of your family members
- Names of your relatives
- Names of your friends
- Names of your colleagues
- Names of your teachers
- Names of your role models
- Names of gods and goddesses
- Sportspersons
- Film actors
- Politicians
- Award winners/scientists/authors
- Fictitious characters

Conditions in Personalized Memory Power System

1. Create the categories in a particular order so that it becomes easy to recollect.
2. Do not mix the categories to maintain clarity.
3. Write the names of those people whose contexts can help bring in some emotions.
4. Do not repeat the names.

5. Remember the name of the person and the corresponding number.
6. Add your own categories.
7. Arrange the categories in a particular order so that it will become easy to recollect.
8. You can assign all odd numbers to women and even numbers to men or vice versa. This will make your job of recollecting much easier.
9. In case there are only three members in a particular category, you may add one more person to the list.
10. In case there are more than four members in a category, omit one person and take only the first three persons.
11. It would be advisable to have a list up to 100 numbers. The way to create names and numbers is categorizing family or friends.

Category: Family—Own
1. Mother
2. Father
3. Sister
4. Brother
5. Grandmother—1
6. Grandfather—1
7. Aunt—1
8. Uncle—1
9. Aunt—2
10. Uncle—2

Category: Family—Extended
1. Grandmother—2
2. Grandfather—2
3. Aunt—3

4. Uncle—3
5. Cousin—1

Category: Friends

1. Cousin—2
2. Childhood Friend—1
3. Childhood Friend—2
4. Classmate—1
5. Classmate—2

Category: Film Actors

1.
2.
3.
4.
5.
6.
7.
8.
9.
10.

Category: Cricket Team

1.
2.
3.
4.
5.
6.
7.
8.

9.
10.

Category: Sportpersons

1.
2.
3.
4.
5.
6.
7.
8.
9.
10.
11.
12.
13.
14.
15.

Category: Role Models

1.
2.
3.
4.
5.

Category: Politicians

1.
2.
3.

4.
5.
6.
7.
8.
9.
10.

Category: Colleagues/Neighbours/Relatives

1.
2.
3.
4.
5.
6.
7.
8.
9.
10.

Category: Teachers

1.
2.
3.
4.
5.
6.
7.
8.
9.
10.

Category: Gods and Goddesses

1.
2.
3.
4.
5.
6.
7.
8.
9.
10.

The first task is to prepare the list of 100 names in a particular order. Then, memorize their names and numbers in order. You should be so perfect in doing this that by recalling any number, you should be able to name the person associated with it instantly. On the other hand, you should be able to recall the name if the number is called out. After doing this, the next task is to associate the objects with the persons. For example, telephone with the first person, Pepsi with the second, popcorn with the third, train with the fourth, and so on. Once you have associated the person with the object, you will be able to recall the objects using numbers and numbers using objects. You will also be able to recall them in ascending or descending order. This is by far the most potent and powerful memory method I have found. You can easily memorize 100 objects with this method. Most of the athletes use this method for memorizing words in the World Memory Championships too.

TWENTY-ONE

MEMORIZING DEFINITIONS, EQUATIONS AND FORMUALE

The actual purpose of education is to understand and not really reproduce what has been internalized. Yet, often, you come across some parts of texts, which need to be reproduced as given in the textbook. Especially, for the sake of examinations, we need to remember equations, formulae and theorems on our fingertips. When you go for competitive examinations all the parameters are given. All that you need to do is to substitute them in the formula and find out the result.

In such situations, mechanical methods come handy. Mechanical means routine or repetition. This is also known as Rote Memory, cramming or remembering by heart. Repetition is the mother of memory. Whether you understand or not, when you repeat something often, you remember it automatically.

That is how we memorized rhymes when we were kids; that is how our grandmothers remember the Gayatri Mantra or the Hanuman Chalisa; that is how a priest in the temple or a church remembers his prayers. This method can work for students as well.

This method is used to memorize: definitions, equations, formulae, statements, constants, quotations, facts, poems, slokas, mantras, pujas or any other text (whichever is not possible to memorize by visualization method), which you have to replicate from textbooks or you need to have on your fingertips.

You need to learn three things to use in this method effectively:

(a) When to start

Most students do not start studying from the first day of their school or college. They keep delaying it and begin only a few days before the exam. Since the brain has a limitation as to how much it can remember by rote method per day, a lot of pressure is put on it, which in turn leads to physical and mental problems.

Last moment preparations lead to a confused state of mind. For example, subject matter may get mixed up, you might forget what you read or you may recollect things that are irrelevant to a subject. You will feel anxious, lose sleep and appetite and begin to sweat profusely.

Hence, if at all you have to use rote memory, you must begin from the first day of school or college. You should pace your studies in such a way that the brain is given enough opportunity to remember.

(b) What to remember

Most of us want to remember everything by rote method without understanding. It is of no use. You might get a good score, but simply reproducing what you have learnt without understanding the concepts is not going to help you at all. Hence, only those things which you do not have to understand but from the examination point of view need to learn, should be memorized by the rote method. Nowadays, in many schools and colleges, the focus is on reproducing rather than understanding the concepts. Due to such measures, students are under a lot of pressure and stress which leads them to dislike studies.

(c) How to remember

Repetition does not mean sitting at home and repeating something n number times. Rather it is about repeating whenever you get spare time.

I use the two following methods:

1. Small scribbling pad

In most stationery shops, you will find small scribbling pads. You can extract all those formulae, equations and whatever your teacher taught and write them out in a scribbling pad. You may have one scribbling pad per subject and to keep one handy every day. You may keep it in your uniform pocket or in your school or college bag's outer pocket.

Use this whenever you get a few minutes of leisure. For example, when you are ready to go to school but the breakfast is yet to be ready, you can scan through a few pages of the scribbling pad, or when you are at the bus stop but the bus has not arrived, you can use this time to revise some of the formulae in your scribbling pad.

You are inside the bus; instead of whiling away your time talking, you can revise.

Your lunch break is 45-minutes long and you are left with a few minutes after lunch; you can use this time for revision.

You are waiting at the clinic for a doctor's appointment; you can make use of this time too.

You are waiting for a friend to meet you; put this time to use.

You are at the movie theatre and still there is half an hour more for the show to begin. Use this time to go through that scribbing pad.

There are only 24 hours in a day and everybody wants to excel in whatever he or she does. Most people sleep and wake up almost at the same time. But unknowingly, we end up wasting a lot of time. The point of focus is on making use of this time. Time is life and life is time. Everyone has limited time on this planet and you need to make the best use of every second and every minute. Studying, excelling in exams and getting to the top is such a serious thing that you cannot afford to waste even a single minute. Hence this technique will work in revising a few formulae at least two times in a day. The next day, take some other book and do the same thing. This way, if you have seven subject areas, you will get to repeat all the formulae once a week. Eventually, you will know them by heart.

2. Chart paper on the wall

Put up lots of coloured chart papers all over the house. In every chart paper, write 40 to 50 formulae. Paste these chart papers next to the mirror in the washroom, to the washroom door, next to the TV, on the kitchen wall, opposite your dining table, in your study room, bedroom, balcony and drawing room, the door leading to the main hall and next to the dressing table.

There are two kinds of reading. One is active reading and the other is passive reading. Active reading is when you decide to sit and study as per the timetable.

Passive reading is when you do not have any fixed time and there is no intention to study. But as you walk inside your house, you get to see the formulae as hoardings, billboards and big banners on the road. Nobody intentionally goes out to read all the hoardings, but when you are stuck in traffic, you tend to see big hoardings and they stay in your memory.

Similarly, when you are in the washroom, at the dining table, resting in the balcony, sitting in the drawing room or dressing up, you tend to see these charts and the content in them stay in your memory.

I used this method when I did my engineering to memorize formulae. I also used this method to memorize the leading particulars of the Aircraft when I was part of the Indian Air Force. I was successful in doing so and I am sure this will work for you as well.

How to Remember by Understanding

The limitation with the mechanical or repetition method is that as long as you have the small scribbling pad or chart papers in the house, you will remember all the formulae. However, the moment you stop revising from the small scribbling pad, you might begin to forget. This means that the remembering by heart method is temporary and will help you to get through the examination. But your actual purpose of study is to understand the concepts and apply them in your daily life, which in turn leads to innovation.

This is possible through the judicious method which involves remembering by understanding. This method can be effectively used to memorize all the science subjects, mathematics, engineering, medicine, computer flow charts or anywhere you need to understand the concepts for higher application and remember information for a long time.

For example, the population problem of India, democracy and how it functions, the election process of the president of USA, how raw iron becomes stainless steel, monsoon cycle, photosynthesis, the digestive process, the computer flow diagrams or anything that you need to understand, this method can be used.

This method is also called Five Wives and One Husband technique. Five Wives means, the five Ws—who, where, when, what and Why. One Husband means, one H—How. Any answer to any question falls under these five headings only.

You have to ask who did it, when did it happen, where did it happen, why was it done, what happened and how it happened.

If you know the answers to all the above five questions, it means you have understood the entire concept and you will be able to answer all questions asked.

This will enhance your thinking and creative skills and will lead to further innovations and success in life. You must encourage your children to follow this method and find out answers for themselves through this process of questions, investigation and exploration.

This will make your knowledge permanent in your brain.

TWENTY-TWO

MEMORIZING LONG SPEECHES

According to a survey that was published a few years ago, the primary fear among human beings is glossophobia—fear of public speaking. The next is the fear of death! When you give a speech without notes, it builds your credibility and self-esteem. When you maintain eye contact, the people you address are impressed with your hold over the subject matter.

I had conducted a five-day 'Train Your Brain' seminar and did not use a single note during my speeches. That is four hours a day and a total of twenty hours a week. I do not memorize my speeches. I file the major thoughts in my files and move from one file to the other so I do not have to recall the speech word by word. Instead, I use brain triggers to move from one file to the next.

I will give you ten pictures. File these in your house files. Use only the first of two rooms as you have just ten pictures. These ten pictures are actually ten items from a speech given on time management. Remember to use your house files.

Here are the items from the speech on time management. Memorize these as quickly as you can.

1. Wall clock
2. Organizer or day planner
3. To-do list
4. Goalpost

5. VIP (Abdul Kalam)
6. Delhi Gate (a nickname you could give to India Gate in Delhi)
7. Joker
8. Calendar
9. Work room
10. Blueprints with glue

You know the drill; write these down and see how many you can get right. Remember that you only need to write the picture down, not the action or the files. How did you do? Did you get all of them?

When you give a speech without referring to notes, you never memorize it word to word. Instead, you have brain triggers to keep you moving from one thought to the next. Here are ten brain triggers that will get us talking about ten major points.

- **Number one:** You open your speech with the subject to be discussed—time management. Thus, the clock becomes the first file.
- **Number two:** An organizer. The word you want to talk about is 'being organized'. After seeing this prompt on your file, you can go into more detail about using a day timer.
- **Number three:** A to-do list. Talk to your group about the importance of writing out a to-do list every day. That way, you can plan your day and become more organized.
- **Number four:** A goal post. You must set and establish goals to be met. At this point, you may mention the importance of setting goals with a deadline and clearly define objectives.
- **Number five:** VIP (Very Important Person—Abdul Kalam). This represents the word importance. This is

- **Number six:** Imagine Delhi Gate (the India Gate in Delhi). The word you want to recall is delegate. Use Delhi and Gate (represents delegate). So, you need to talk about how to delegate work.
- **Number seven:** Joker. When you see this, remind your audience that it is important to set time aside for fun. Allocate time to let your mind relax and have some fun.
- **Number eight:** Calendar—a schedule. When you see the calendar, it will remind you of the importance of keeping a fixed schedule—waking up at the same time every day and preparing a routine.
- **Number nine:** You are going to talk about setting up a special room to work in. This is a place where you can get away from all distractions and focus on work.
- **Number ten:** This is a blueprint with glue on it. You review your speech and recap the highlights, reinforce to your audience the importance of having a plan and sticking to it. That is what the glue symbolizes.

Now, you understand the concept of how to give a speech without notes. It is not important to memorize every word. Just create brain triggers and then file them. Giving speeches without notes is an exclusive skill, and one that will increase your confidence when you master it.

The same technique can be used for giving sales presentation or any presentation without using notes. This is a money-making skill and can be done within minutes. The trick is to assign keywords to each paragraph or to the logical part of the speech and then list out the keywords to link it to the speech. This way you will always know what to talk about.

Perhaps you have heard about Thomas Edison. It took him over thousand attempts to invent the light bulb. After he successfully created the light bulb, he held a press conference and a brash reporter asked him, 'Mr. Edison, how does it make you feel to have failed over ten thousand times?' Mr Edison, without missing a beat, promptly responded, 'You misunderstand. I did not fail over ten thousand times. I successfully found ten thousand ways how not to invent electric bulb.'

Now, that is a positive attitude and it is an attitude that you can learn from for sure. If you do not get a perfect score, do what Mr Edison did; try and try till you succeed.

The file system I use to give my presentation involve my skeleton files. That is where we are going to store a sales presentation. Let us say that you are a salesperson who would like to nail your presentation down a little better. You need to break it down into separate thoughts, then turn those thoughts into pictures and file them into your files.

I am going to give you ten items you need to scan through quickly. These items are going to represent the steps in a sales presentation. Most companies have a presentation that at the end has a call for action, and the presentation is designed in a specific manner. After you do this exercise, you should have a good understanding of a very practical business application to this system that we are about to learn.

File these pictures to your files as fast as you can.

1. Handshake for the introduction
2. Statistics
3. Professional giving an opinion
4. Asking questions
5. Filling a need
6. Demonstration

7. Features and benefits
8. Testimonials or third party references
9. Investment
10. Call to action

Okay, scan through it one more time if you have to and then write these ten items down. How did you do? If you got all ten, give yourself a pat on the back. If you missed one, ask yourself why. Did you know your file and was your picture vivid enough? Give yourself some credit if you scored well. Remember, if you have assigned ten pictures rapidly and then recited them forwards, backwards and by number, you will be very impressed. That is what you just did.

Now, I will file these words in my skeleton files. Whether you are just learning to remember a presentation or you are a veteran at it, this technique will come handy. Remember that when you see a young salesperson struggling to learn the steps of the presentation, tell him or her to build files in his office and then use pictures as brain triggers.

In this situation, what you would do is file these ten major points. If there is more information that you want to file, associate these additional words to more files.

TWENTY-THREE

MEMORIZING MONTHS AND DAYS

You have learnt how to remember the numbers. By using this number technique, you can memorize years. However, at times, in a competitive examination, you have to remember the days and months also. The following method will help you memorize months and days.

Months

There are 12 months in a year. Many a times, you need to remember the month someone was born in, or an event that took place or when a particular day is celebrated. You know how to convert the years into images with the help of the phonetic method. You might get stuck when it comes to months. Most of us do not really know what to do. Here is the clue for memorizing months.

I have developed the following codes for different months:

January	–	New Year party—imagine celebration
February	–	Valentine's Day—imagine roses
March	–	Planet Mars
April	–	April Fool's Day—imagine a joker in a circus
May	–	May Day—imagine a labourer
June	–	School starting—imagine school
July	–	First unit test—imagine writing an exam
August	–	Independence Day—Indian flag

September	–	Soap bar—imagine washing clothes using a soap bar
October	–	Octopus
November	–	Children day—imagine a Child
December	–	Christmas—imagine Jesus Christ

You have to imagine the pictures above. You can replace them with something more meaningful or personal to you.

Days

There are seven days in a week. What if someone asks you to remember the days?

Imagine you had been to some place on a particular day or there was an event on a weekday. As of now, it is difficult to remember these days. This might help you to remember them.

The way you have developed codes for the months, you can do the same for the days as well.

Monday	–	Monitor (imagine a computer monitor) or going to office
Tuesday	–	Toast—preparing bread toast
Wednesday	–	Wood—imagine a lovely forest
Thursday	–	Thermometer
Friday	–	Fruit—imagine an orange
Saturday	–	Star Fish
Sunday	–	Holiday—imagine snow or going for a picnic

TWENTY-FOUR

MEMORIZING CALENDARS

5 January 1965—What day was it?

Now, you will have to fall back on the calendar or get onto the Internet. But you do not have to do this anymore.

To tell any day from the date, you need to know the date, month and year. Once these are provided, you will be able to instantly tell the day using the following method, which I use.

There are two parts to the whole calendar memorization.

First Part: Calculate using a formula.
Second Part: Memory

Procedure to calculate the day for the date:

Day code + Month Code + Year Code = Total/7.
Find out the remainder.
If the remainder is …
1–Sunday, 2–Monday, 3–Tuesday, 4–Wednesday, 5–Thursday, 6– Friday, 0–Saturday

If adding the date, month and year codes gives a total that is less than seven, do not divide it by seven. You must take the total itself as the remainder and can simply tell the day, using the above formula.

In case of a leap year, subtract one day from the remainder only for the months of January and February (1 January to 29 February). For example, if the remainder is 2 (Monday), subtract a day from it. Therefore, the answer will be the day before the remainder calculated using the formula above.

Memorizing the codes

Date code: Date itself

Month Code

January–1	May–2	September–6
February–4	June–5	October–1
March–4	July–0	November–4
April–0	August–3	December–6

Year code (Standard century from 1901–2000)

1901–1	1921–5	1941–2	1961–6	1981–3
1902–2	1922–6	1942–3	1962–0	1982–4
1903–3	1923–0	1943–4	1963–1	1983–5
1904–5	1924–2	1944–6	1964–3	1984–0
1905–6	1925–3	1945–0	1965–4	1985–1
1906–0	1926–4	1946–1	1966–5	1986–2
1907–1	1927–5	1947–2	1967–6	1987–3
1908–3	1928–0	1948–4	1968–1	1988–5
1909–4	1929–1	1949–5	1969–2	1989–6
1910–5	1930–2	1950–6	1970–3	1990–0
1911–6	1931–3	1951–0	1971–4	1991–1
1912–1	1932–5	1952–2	1972–6	1992–3
1913–2	1933–6	1953–3	1973–0	1993–4
1914–3	1934–0	1954–4	1974–1	1994–5
1915–4	1935–1	1955–5	1975–2	1995–6

1916–6	1936–3	1956–0	1976–4	1996–1
1917–0	1937–4	1957–1	1977–5	1997–2
1918–1	1938–5	1958–2	1978–6	1998–3
1919–2	1939–6	1959–3	1979–0	1999–4
1920–4	1940–1	1960–5	1980–2	2000–6
2001–0	2005–5	2009–3	2013–1	2017–6
2002–1	2006–6	2010–4	2014–2	2018–0
2003–2	2007–0	2011–5	2015–3	2019–1
2004–4	2008–2	2012–0	2016–4	2020–3

Century's code

All the calculations are based on this standard century.

If you know the codes from 1901 to 2000, you will be able to go forward a century or back a century.

Let us go forward a century:

1901–2000—Standard Century for example, 1901–X

2001–onwards—subtract 1 from the standard century (2001 = X–1)

Since the code for 1901 is 1, the code for 2001 will become 0 (1–1= 0)

Let us go back in century:

The code for 1901 is 1. If we go back a century, we have to add 2 to the particular code.

1801 – 3 (1+2=3)

Let us go back one more century:

If the code for 1901 is 1, for the code of 1701, you need to add 4:

1701 – 5 (1+4=5)

Let us go back one more century:

If the code for 1901 is 1, for the code of 1601, you need to add 6 more:

1601 − 0 (1+6=0)

 **Exercise:**

1. 05 January 1965
   5+1+4 =10/7 = Remainder 3 (Tuesday)
2. 17 May 1996
   17+2+1=20/7 = Remainder 6 (Friday)
3. 18 Jan 1999
   18+1+4=23/7= Remainder 2 (Monday)

Can you also calculate and find out your birthday, wedding day or any other day? Did you get it right! Great! This will need some practice. So, practise and revise.

TWENTY-FIVE

MEMORIZING TO-DO LISTS AND ROAD DIRECTIONS

Remembering 'To-do Things'

Why is it so difficult to remember 'to-do things'? In fact, they are more difficult to remember than events. The primary reason is the lack of retrieval cues. This is why, of all memory tasks, to remember 'to-do things' relies most heavily on external memory aids like notes, calendars, diaries, watch alarms, mobile alarms, organizers, laptops, etc.

In partial compensation for the lack of effective retrieval cues, planning memories are more easily triggered by minor cues. I was reminded to buy a train ticket as I passed by a railway station.

When you wish for something, you usually link it to either an event or a time. But these triggered events or times frequently fail to remind you of your intention. Sometimes, the trigger itself is not distinct.

I want you to start to file your to-do list to your files. Always start from the top. Remember to use your files whenever you go through the process during the day. Let us say you have five things to do, and someone calls to remind you throughout the day: 'Do not forget to call Ram!' Your picture for Ram is of Lord Rama. So, you immediately file that in your next open file. When you complete a task in your files, change the picture, set it on fire, throw it into the water or tick it off with a big red checkmark.

Else, make a list of all things to be done for the next one year. For example, payment of car insurance, health check-up, planning a holiday, wishing someone on his or her birthday or wedding anniversary, an important appointment, writing a book, building a house, payment of child's school fee, etc.

Thereafter, at the end of every month, make a list of to-do things.

Every Sunday, make a list of to-do things for the next one week.

From thereon, before you sleep, make a list of to-do things on priority basis on a piece of paper and keep that paper in your shirt's pocket.

Every day, when you reach office, check things that are to be done and keep ticking them off on an hourly basis.

When you make a list of to-do things at the end of the day for the next day, check from this list if you have left behind anything incomplete and transfer them to the new list.

This is an effective way of getting things done.

Also, learn to do usual things in an unusual way.

For example, I have to go the bank early in the morning to make a deposit. What I normally do is wear my watch on my the left arm instead of my right. I usually wear my watch on my left hand. The fact that I am wearing it on my right makes me very uncomfortable, as if I am carrying something heavy. When I look at the time, I wonder why I am wearing the watch on my right hand. This unusual act reminds me of something important I need to do, that is, going to the bank.

Secondly, imagine I am supposed to book my train ticket on Tatkal the following day, but I am scared that I might forget. What I do is to take out my handkerchief from my pocket. Normally, I fold the handkerchief and keep it in the pocket. But today, I make few knots in it and keep it in my pocket. When I reach office, the moment I have a glass of water or a cup of coffee, the reflective action is to take out the handkerchief from my pocket. I find it in knots. This is unusual and it reminds me that I am supposed to book my train tickets on Tatkal.

Ladies may choose to go without a bindi on their forehead, leave their hair untied or do something different and unusual. These strange actions will remind you of what you need to do.

Besides, you have to be confident that you indeed have a very good memory and you will start doing everything perfectly. This self-confidence will automatically enhance your memory.

Remembering Road Directions

What about directions? Have you ever stopped and asked somebody for directions and then you cannot remember what the person said? For example, if they say, 'Go down to M.G. Road and take a left and cross two stop signs and take a right. Go to King Street and take a left and you are there.' You drive away thinking, 'Great!' and then you cannot recall what the directions were. This is because rights and lefts are abstract. Here is something you can do to recall directions.

Assign the red colour to every right and 'full of leaves' to every left. Assign an 'umbrella' to a U-turn. When someone says, 'Go down to M.G. Road and take a left,' file Mahatma Gandhi covered with 'leaves' in your first file. Then the person said, 'Cross two stop signs and make a right.' File two stop signs and the red colour in your next file. Moving ahead, you were instructed to 'Go to King Street and take a left.' File the king's crown 'full of leaves' to file number three. If you were told to go straight to the Hanuman Mandir and take a U-turn, imagine Lord Hanuman holding an Umbrella and place it in the next file. You are simply turning abstracts into pictures.

You normally either walk forward, take a left turn, then make a right turn or a U-turn. As long as we drive straight ahead, there is nothing to imagine. When you need to take a U-turn, imagine an umbrella covering the landmark. When you take a right turn, imagine red colour paint over that landmark. When you have to take left turn, imagine a lot of dry leaves covering that a landmark. Now, you will not miss any directions. This will also take some practice, but it becomes very simple once you get it.

TWENTY-SIX

MEMORIZING NAMES AND FACES

Often, you meet people at a railway station, airport, meeting or a family function. You meet people whom you have never met before and familiarize yourself with their names and appearances. Next time, you meet them in a shopping mall or at some other function, you know you have met them, but cannot recollect their names. You are embarrassed when they approach you because since you do not remember their names and do not know how to respond.

Has this ever happened to you? If yes, then here is a technique that will help you to remember the names and faces of people.

Why Do You Need to Remember Names and Faces of People?

Irrespective of the Memory Competition, in real life too, people are expected to remember names and faces of others. A person's name is the sweetest sound to another in any language. People generally love their names. If you remember and call them by their names, they generally respond in a similar manner. This means for a relationship, the starting point is calling a person by his/her name. Hence, for any leader or businessperson, memorizing names will definitely help them succeed in life. It is the first step towards building good human relations with people around.

If Names Are Important, Why Do We Not Remember Them?

When someone is telling his or her name, people are busy thinking how they could introduce themselves in a better way than the other just did. They do not pay attention, hence do not register, and therefore, will not be able to recall the name.

Sometimes, people take it very casually or do not care enough to value the other person. Hence, they pretend as if they are listening but they are not really doing so. So the next time if they need to recall the names, they are unable to do so.

Let us discuss a three-step formula to remember names of people.

Step 1

Impression

Whenever you meet a new person, imagine that there is a traffic signal behind him or her. The traffic signal will have three lights: red, amber (yellow) and green. First, see the red light, which means stop thinking, free your mind and pay attention to the person. Yellow light means observe the physical features of the person. How tall, short, fat, thin, fair, dark, the colour of his or her hair and observe any other special or striking features that person has. You may have to notice the face, nose, mouth, ears, cheeks, hair, forehead and other parts of his body and try to make out something that stands out or is unusual. Imprint this feature in the mind and you have to link the name of the person to it. When you look at the person keenly, your subconscious mind will take a picture of the person and store it. The next time you see the person, the picture comes flashing and you know that you have met this person before.

Step 2

Repetition

As discussed earlier, repetition is the mother of Memory. Repeat the newly heard name as many times as possible. In real life, when you try to call a person by his or her name, the tongue gets used to saying this name and that lodges it into your subconscious mind. Also, be careful when you listen to the name—the pronunciation and its meaning—and get it right. When you ask for names, most people say them in a low voice, which is difficult to catch. Secondly, if they happen to be from a different country, region, religion or culture, it becomes further difficult as you have never come across these names. Hence, you have to make sure that you have heard the name and repeat it three or four times in the conversation with the person: once, at the beginning of the sentence, then, in the middle, and finally, at the end without the other person noticing. In this way, the name is embedded in the memory and you will be able to recall the name easily later.

Step 3

Association

As the person is leaving the place, associate the newly heard person's name with somebody or something you already know. Always link the new with the old or unknown with the known; that is how you expand your horizon of knowledge and memory base.

The problem is that when you hear the name and you do not see the name. Seeing is more powerful than hearing. How you see the name converts the name into an image, you could also associate this name with somebody you already know.

If someone says, his name is Ram. Then, imagine Lord Rama

drinking a cup of coffee or sitting with the famous lawyer like Ram Jethmalani.

You may also clearly observe the face and pick up some salient or distinct feature on it like the mouth, eyes, nose, ears, hair, forehead; the dress one is wearing; whether the person is male/female, young/old, etc.

Then, go through the name. Every name will have a first name and the second name. The names could be Indian or from a different origin. That does not matter. You have to break the word and make a meaning out of it and associate this name with the face of the person. Suppose I come across the name Suresh. Maybe I will break this and remember as 'shoe-race'. You can break Karthik into a person driving a car and making a 'ticking' sound. If you have a name Anil, connect this name with Anil Ambani, Anil Kumble, Anil Kapoor or any other person who you know.

A little bit of practice and it will help you master this skill of memorizing names and faces of people. Just by calling somebody by his or her name, you can create such a great impact on that person.

This technique will be very useful for people who are in business, politics, have an active public life, into management or just in general. Remembering names accurately is a great skill that is very useful in day to day life.

TWENTY-SEVEN

REINFORCING AND REVIEWING

Many people complain about gradually forgetting what they read. You have to understand that it is quite natural to forget. Imagine that you remember all that you have read, written, said, listened, done, experienced or visited. Your life will become really difficult to live.

Hence, the brain has been designed to remember and forget. In fact, forgetting is more important than remembering. If you do not forget, then all your tensions and worries will really make your life miserable. You are able to forget, hence you are able to live happily.

On the contrary, students often say that it is OK to forget bad things. But, they will need to remember what they read and learn forever.

Even though you are aware of this, your brain is not. As a matter of routine, anything that we might have learnt but do not use, the brain will automatically forget.

Hence, if you have to remember studies until exams get over, you should reinforce the matter and review at regular intervals.

The two key techniques to accelerate your learning are reinforcing and reviewing.

Reinforcing

Whatever you learn, say, right after you have had a lesson, you should write it down or recall what you just learnt after 5–10 minutes. This reinforces the learning and improves your ability to recall it later. If you do not do this, the lesson will quickly fade from your memory. You will not forget everything, but you will neither remember anywhere near to as much as you would by making some quick notes.

You DO NOT have to write an encyclopedia. Sometimes just a single word will do. No one understands you better than you do! Which bit of the lesson did you struggle with? Which bit do you think you will have trouble remembering? Write THAT down!

Do not worry about getting it right 100 per cent. If you learnt something new, but you cannot remember it, just write it down in the best way you can. You can always fix it later if you need to. Writing down something wrong is better than not writing down anything at all.

Next thing you should do is continue reading a chapter, theorem or concept for 4 days. If you have read a chapter today, you must reinforce it over the next three days by revising the same thing. This impression will stay longer.

Reviewing

Next thing you should do is to take out some time and review what you have learnt once in a fortnight. This will ensure that what you have learnt stays in your memory. You have to make a timetable in such a manner that half the subjects come for revision every week so that you keep on reinforcing what you have learnt.

You should skim over your notes periodically. How often you should do this is up to you, but I find that once a week works well for me. The better you know the material, the less often you have to review it. Things from a year ago may only need reviewing every three months, but something difficult that you just learnt might need reviewing every day until you start to understand it.

It is also worth reviewing right before a lesson. If you are anything like I am, you will spend the first 5-10 minutes of any lesson trying to remember where you were in the previous lesson.

Tools for Reinforcing and Reviewing

Stated below are some best tools for reinforcing and reviewing.

Paper-based

This is the simplest option. Just buy a little notebook, and write into it. Use a page per subject. The biggest disadvantages to this option are that you cannot easily edit what you have written on it or search something you are looking for specifically. Despite the disadvantages, this is still a good option, and definitely worth considering if you do not have access to a computer.

Word Processor

This option requires a computer. Just use any standard Word Processor (even Microsoft Notepad would do), and type your notes into it. You may want to have different subjects in different files; otherwise, the files will get very long. This option has advantages over paper, because you can edit and search for specific things easily.

Improve Memory Up To 10 Times

I am going to give you some hints on how to use memory techniques to make things easier to remember. I will only explain each thing in one sentence just to give you a general idea. When you use memory techniques, you eliminate rote memory. No rote memory is needed; only imagination will suffice. The best part with remembering things with memory techniques is interesting and you have extra motivation to do so.

Link Mechanism

Remembering shopping lists or long lists of items with memory techniques is a breeze. What you need to do is associate each item with the next one in the list. You need to associate the two items in some unusual way that stays in your mind.

Repetition

This is a very simple technique and probably the most used to remember something. However, look closely at what you are really doing when you are repeating something. You are forcing yourself to pay attention to something. That is one of the most important steps in memorization. You forget most things simply because you did not remember them in the first place.

Storytelling

The Greeks were great at storytelling. They would take phenomena from everyday events and weave a story around it. By creating a story they are forcing your attention (see how important that is) plus they are creating a link mechanism which I mentioned above. All good memory techniques play off each other and use the brain's natural memory ability. Remember that these are techniques, not tricks!

Rhyming

Admittedly, it takes some creative energy and a talent for forming rhymes, but if you have that ability, it is a very good way to remember things. The rhyme can have a story as well.

Association

Associate one item to something you already know. Remember how memory works. How often a smell can bring back the memory of a certain lunch you had with a friend a long time ago. Association is a way that was devised to utilize the way memory naturally works. You are not forcing it, but it is something you do naturally.

TWENTY-EIGHT

OVERCOMING ABSENT-MINDEDNESS OR FORGETFULNESS

Many people often complain that they are having absent-mindedness or forgetfulness. In the sense that they forget where they have kept their house or vehicle keys, helmet, spectacles, pen, purse or mobile phones. Some women also complain that they keep the milk on the gas stove and forget to turn the stove off, leave the washroom geyser switched on or forget to switch off the lights and fans.

The first thing that we have to understand is that forgetfulness is not equal to not having a good memory. You may have very good memory but you can still forget. We generally use the term, 'Absent-minded Professor'. It means, a professor remembers many things, from the textbooks and guide research students, but forgets where he had left the attendance register. This happens because the professor's total attention is on research and teaching, and he is unable to pay much attention to small things. This means, when you are fully preoccupied or immersed in a big task like running a business, starting a company, getting the school to function, politics or busy organizing a family wedding, your complete attention is on getting the bigger things done and you do not pay attention to the smaller ones. Hence, people forget. Most often people say they are suffering from absent-mindedness.

If you belong to this category, the solution is very simple.

Overcoming Absent-mindedness or Forgetfulness • 153

Have an assistant or a secretary to take care of small things so that you will never complain about forgetting things.

The next thing is that people will not pay attention when you are doing things. The reason being 95 per cent of the time, human beings either live in the past or are worried about their future, and hence, never live in the present. Most of us are busy thinking something else while keeping a pen in the cupboard drawer. The next time you want the pen, you know that you kept it somewhere, but where? Not able to recall as the mind was absent during the moment you kept it.

Hence, the idea is to live in the moment. One has to understand the power of 'now'. When you learn to live in the moment, life seems so beautiful and you will have no worries; there is no feeling of envy or jealousy.

The next problem is that most of you want to do everything yourself in a day. You want to get milk from the shop, take the dog for walk, give the car for servicing, book railway tickets, pay up electricity bills, buy provisions, vegetables and take care of office work. You should know that our brain can only do so much. When you give too much work to the brain, you tend to forget one or two things and people do perceive this as forgetfulness. You can overcome this problem by prioritizing all the work you need to get done. Let people do what they can; you do what nobody can. Thereby meaning, you need to find out the difference in profit when you delegate work to someone and when you do it yourself. You should take up whichever gives you more profit. Hence, once you prioritize work and keep your mind free of stress, you will be able to remember everything.

The next thing people complain about is that they forget their watch, pen, purse, bike or car keys. This happens because they do not have a fixed place for an item. What they should do is develop a discipline at home for one item in one place. For example, shoes have to be left at the shoe stand, mobile has to go to the charging point, the helmet has to be on the table, your bike/car/office keys have to be in the key bunch, your spectacles, watch, pen and purse should go into the cupboard drawer. If you do any task continuously for 21 days, it will become a habit. If you can develop this habit, you will be able to find your purse, spectacles or keys anytime. Everybody in the house would also know where to find which item.

People often ask me if I have designated places for my belongings at my home, but what do I do when I visit a new place, someone's house or a hotel. In such cases, you must use the imagination/association technique. For example, when you keep the spectacles near the TV set, you have to link both items to form a funny picture in your mind. Here, the TV is wearing spectacles. When you keep the purse under your pillow, imagine that the pillow is full of money. You will be able to recall where you kept the items by visualizing and associating both images.

Has it ever happened to you that someone asked you to bring a book from home and you forgot? But, the moment you saw the person in the office, you remembered about the book? Similarly, as you leave home, your spouse asks you to buy bananas and you forget after reaching office. The moment you have reached home in the evening and see your spouse you know that you have forgotten the bananas.

You can overcome this problem by the reminder technique. You remembered the book when you saw your friend in the office. Imagine that you saw your friend when you stepped out of the house; will you forget the book? No.

Similarly, you remembered the bananas once you saw your spouse at the door. Imagine you happened to see your spouse at the car park before you drove out, will you then forget bananas? No.

This principle can be applied in the reminder technique.

What you need to do is to have one checkpoint at the exit door of your house and another checkpoint at the car park area of your office. If somebody asks you to get something from home, keep his or her pictures or objects at the exit door of your house. Every day, when you leave the house, you have to stop for a second at the exit door and recollect what all you need to take to office. Once you leave the house, just mentally wipe off those images from the door. When somebody from the house asks you to get something on your way back from office, imagine his or her pictures and objects or things related to these people at the checkpoint next to your car parking area. It should become a habit for you that as you are about to start your vehicle, you must look at the checkpoint and ensure that you have everything you need. Now, you will not forget anything to take back home.

Sometimes, you forget to carry a gift on your way to a wedding. At times, you forget the train ticket back home. This is because you go through motions of life without thinking. Before you get up from any place, you have to sit quietly for a few seconds and ask the following questions:

Who am I?
Where am I going?
Why am I going?
What do I need to carry?

From there, you again need to think:

What all do I need to do?
Where do I need to go?
Whom am I supposed to meet?

When you ask these questions, you know that you have to go to a wedding. Therefore, you will definitely carry the gift, your travel tickets, clothes, toiletries and other required items. Similarly, as you leave that place, ask these questions: What all did I bring with me? Am I carrying everything or am I leaving behind anything? I usually do this ahead of a journey. I am sure this will work for you too.

Let Us Use Our Biological Clock

When women complain that they forget about the simmering milk on the gas stove or leave the lights/fans/geyser switched on, this is because they do not use their biological clock.

When I was a kid, my grandfather used to tell me before sleeping that he needed to get up by 4.00 a.m. to water the paddy fields. Surprisingly, he would get up exactly at that hour. In those days, the concept of alarm clocks was not there. I often wondered how he managed to get up exactly at the same time every day. Later, I understood that before going to sleep, he told himself that he is supposed to get up by 4.00 a.m. This signal would go to every cell of his body and by 4.00 a.m. the body would automatically wake him up. This is called the biological clock. I experienced the same thing recently. I was supposed to go to the airport to pick up my sister who was coming from USA after two years at 3.00 a.m. I set the mobile alarm at 1.30 a.m. But, I woke up much before the alarm went off. This is because I told myself before going to sleep that I have to get up by 1.30 a.m. This works. Hence, when you are place the milk on the stove to boil, you must tell yourself that you are doing so and you should turn it off in another 10 minutes. You will be amazed that no matter where you are or with whom you are, your body will automatically remind you to turn the stove off. Same is the case with the geyser or tap in the washroom. You must be conscious and alert when you are at work and tell yourself what the next thing to be done is. The body will act as a reminder for you.

Another scenario that you might face is say you are going

out for a seminar and it is raining very heavily. So, you carry an umbrella. At the seminar hall, you leave the umbrella outside and attend the seminar. By evening, when the seminar has gotten over, it has stopped raining and you return home while chatting with a friend, you have forgotten about the umbrella. You will never remember that you had forgotten the umbrella until it rains again.

But, let us assume another scenario. You went to the seminar hall with an umbrella as it was raining. You kept the umbrella outside the seminar hall. The seminar got over in the evening. Assume that it was still raining. Now, will you come home without the umbrella? You will not. This means that if the same situation exists when you begin a task and when you end it, you will not forget to carry your belongings with you, but if it changes, you might.

This has happened to me quite a few times when I go for training. I wear a blazer to the training. By lunch, I usually take it off and leave it on the table. In the evening, I am in a hurry to head back home and I never think of the blazer. This is how I lost two blazers. Later, I instructed my subordinate that the moment I take off the blazer, it should go back to my car. Ever since, I have never lost any of my blazers. Similarly, you can also assign someone to take care of the belongings before leaving any place so that you do not miss out on any item.

Most importantly, people say that as they age their ability to remember reduces. This happens because the brain neurons keep receding due to less mental or intellectual activity. The only way they can maintain their mental health and good memory is by living a balanced life, remaining peaceful, meditating, reading, learning new skills, keeping busy and solving puzzles, and participating in intellectual debates and discussions. This will ensure that one is mentally agile even though he or she is growing old physically.

TWENTY-NINE

ERASING BAD MEMORIES

So far, you have learnt about how to remember information. In this chapter, you will learn how to forget.

All of us go through ups and downs in life, we sometimes face success, sometimes failures. Happiness here and sadness there, troubles and tribulations, profits and losses, births and deaths, appreciation and backstabbing—all are a part and parcel of life.

Whenever any activity or event involves emotions of happiness, we act in your usual manner. But when we face hurdles or experience failure, most of us take a long time to recover from them. The reason being that the brain has been designed to remember and forget. And this forgetting is more important than remembering. You can forget, push all the bad memories out of your working memory so that you are able to lead a happy life.

When there is a death in the family or neighbourhood, loss or failure, the intensity of the negative emotion is so high that you are not able to lead the ususal life. Most of you take a break, sit in a corner, stay aloof, go into depression and it takes a long time to bounce back to your normal routine. As you go through the motions of life and get back to daily chores, negative emotions that have affected you gradually fade away. After some time, you are able to watch movies, visit restaurants, attend functions, crack jokes and move ahead in life.

Unfortunately, some people hang on to these negative

emotions or lose so much that they are unable to lead a normal life and ruin the rest of their lives. In case, you are stuck with one such thing, you could try the technique below for erasing bad memories.

You have learnt in the previous chapters how to remember. For any image to be strong and vivid, you have to magnify the picture, visualize it in motion, colour, and in an illogical and funny manner, involve all your senses to do so and build a personal connect.

To forget, you have to follow the same process in the reverse and take out all the above components.

Let us imagine that somebody scolded you, shouted at you or criticized you for no apparent reason. This is repeatedly coming back to your mind and is affecting your mood, hindering you from leading a normal life. Let us see how can you overcome this problem.

Step 1
Sit all alone in a room and close your eyes, take a deep breath and tell yourself to relax, relax and relax.

Imagine that you are in a big movie theatre watching a movie. On the 70 mm screen, try to play the incident that is bothering you, with vivid colours and sounds.

Watch the entire incident from beginning till end. (This way, you have removed the 'personal' element from the memory as you have watched a scene where somebody criticized someone else and not *you*).

Step 2
This time, replay the same incident from the beginning to the end, but remove the colours, turning it into a black and white movie. (Here you have removed the colours from the scene).

Step 3
This time, replay the same incident, but turn off the volume/dialogues. So, you see some people move their lips, but you are not able to hear anything. (Here, you have removed the sound from the situation).

Step 4
Now, replay the incident. This time, turn this incident into a very old, black and white movie of 1960s and 1970s. The clarity and screenplay of these movies were not up to the mark and thus you tend to lose interest in it soon. (Here you have blurred the images in this movie so that your mind loses interest in this incident.)

Step 5
This time, play the black and white, blurred, mute movie once again. Imagine the movie screen is becoming smaller and smaller and moving away from you. Before it vanishes, either imagine holding it in your fist, tearing it into pieces and throwing it away, or throwing some water on that small piece or setting fire to it. You then tell yourself that it is *gone*.

I am sure, this five-step process will help reduce the intensity of the incident that is bothering you and this memory will be erased from your current memory.

Do not give any importance to that incident, do not try to recollect it or be part of a discussion where people may remind you of what happened. This will certainly help you to lead a normal life.

For the last few years that I am in the profession of memory training, people have shared with me their problems and things that they have been unable to forget. I train them using this technique and counsel them to look at life on a larger canvas. You need to train yourself to look at life in a better way.

You may drop a tear or two on certain occasions. That is it.

The problem is that you repeatedly think of the same incident. If I have cracked a joke and you have heard it for the first time, you will laugh out loudly. Just imagine that I cracked the same joke after a few minutes; you will not laugh, but you may smile. After another 15 minutes, if I crack the same joke again, you might look at me thinking that I may have gone mad. The logic is that if you do not laugh at the same joke the second time, why do you cry over the same incident again and again? Cry once and let go. You must learn a lesson and ensure that such an incident does not happen again.

Life is all about looking ahead and not backwards. You cannot change people, what they say or how they act, but you can control the situation by learning how to embrace it. No one can make you happy or sad but you. Understand that life is very short and you live only once and it is good to remember and cherish happy memories rather than hold onto bad ones, cry over them and ruin your life.

I am sure these principles will help you lead a very happy and mentally healthy life.

Keep practising these techniques and keep using them in your day-to-day life and you will see phenomenal results.

FEEDBACK WELCOME

Dear Reader,

If you have enjoyed reading the book, feel free to send us your feedback. On the other hand, if you feel I have left out something important, I would still love to hear from you.

We would also like to find out if this book has inspired you to take any practical steps in your day-to-day life in improving your memory.

You may also contact me for practical training on memory for yourself or your children. You may also get in touch with me for any practical videos, online training, counselling sessions and motivational programs.

I can be reached through my e-mail: **visionjay@gmail.com**, my website **www.jayasimha.in** or my Facebook page: Jayasimha Squadron Leader

Squadron Leader Jayasimha
President World Memory Sports Council for India
Multiple Guinness World Record Holder
Memory Maestro, Trainer, Motivational Speaker